# all about putting

by
the editors of
Golf Digest

illustrated by Dick Kohfield

A Golf Digest Book
Coward, McCann & Geoghegan, Inc., New York

ISBN 0-914178-04-0
Library of Congress Catalog Card
Number: 73-88174
Second printing 1974
Printed in the United States of America.

# all about putting

# contents

# introduction

Putting is the most personal of all golf strokes. Bobby Locke, who many believe is the greatest putter of all time, "hooked" all of his putts, curling them into the cup from right to left. Billy Casper putts with his wrists. Bob Charles locks his wrists and putts with an arms and shoulders stroke. Bobby Jones putted with a combination arm and wrist stroke. There's a fellow named Vance Elkins who putts with his hips. With the possible exception of the latter, no one can question that each of these superstars has been a master putter.

Style and personal idiosyncrasies vary dramatically among golf's great putters, but all of them agree that if a golfer improves his putting game he will reduce his score faster than any other way.

Furthermore, as you will discover while reading this guide to the art and strategy of putting, other phases of your golf game invariably are affected by the putting game, whether for better or worse.

Cary Middlecoff, one of the great putters in history, advised

7

that "any golfer can make himself a better putter if he will approach the problem intelligently and work at it."

This book prescribes no single, set method for knocking a golf ball into the hole. Rather, it presents in detail the various methods and ideas of the game's greatest putters as selected by the editors of Golf Digest magazine. It represents a collection of the soundest, most valuable putting instruction ever assembled.

The experts differ in some respects on putting methods but they are in remarkable agreement that certain basic principles of grip, stance and stroke are essential to successful putting. These points of agreement are gathered together and explained in Chapter 10.

The book stresses the more conventional putting styles and their many variations, and focuses on the putting fundamentals that all golfers should emphasize, whatever their chosen technique may be.

The cross-handed method, whose most notable exponents are Orville Moody and Marilynn Smith, is examined, as is the side-saddle technique of Sam Snead. Also analyzed is the split-handed method used with such conspicuous success by Phil Rodgers, who learned it from Paul Runyan, one of the truly great putters in the history of golf. The Runyan-Rodgers technique calls for placing the right hand well below the left on the shaft—a sort of golfing variation of what is known in baseball as the Ty Cobb grip—and using a putter some two or three inches longer than the norm.

Our purpose is not necessarily to cover the whole range of putting techniques solely for the sake of encyclopedic comprehensiveness. Rather, the basic aim is to help the golfer-reader find something that will help his own putting—if only by confirming or disputing some apparently outlandish theory whose validity he questions.

Any book on putting should stress its importance in the over-all picture of golf. Examples of putting as a major factor of successful golf are many:

In winning two National Opens—in 1959 at Winged Foot in the New York area and at the Olympic Club in San Francisco in 1966—Billy Casper one-putted over 40 per cent of the holes. In the 1966 Open, which went 90 holes because it ended in a tie that forced a playoff between Casper and Arnold Palmer, Casper didn't three-putt a green until the ninth hole of the playoff—the eighty-first hole of the tournament. And when asked at San Francisco when he had last putted so well, Casper replied, "At Winged Foot in 1959." The clear inference is that great putting brings victory, provided the rest of the player's game is comparable to that of the other contenders, which Casper's definitely is. If Casper had just averaged two putts per green in these tournaments, he would not have finished among the first 50 places at either Winged Foot or Olympic.

The above observations merely reflect cold statistics. They show only that good putting lowered Casper's winning scores by the number of times he one-putted instead of two-putted.

No perceptive golfer could doubt that those stroke-saving and nerve-saving one-putt greens kept his confidence and competitive spirit high and thus helped him hit the fine long shots that he needed to reach positions where good putting could make him a winner.

Among others, Gary Player and Cary Middlecoff have maintained that the confidence so vital to low-scoring golf occurs in a sort of reverse pattern, from green to tee.

In much the same vein, Player has commented frequently on the confidence good putting gives a player. The essence of his theory is that when a bad putter makes an approach shot to the green he seldom makes his best shot because, consciously or unconsciously, he believes it won't make that much difference. He doesn't believe he can sink a putt, and so lacks the necessary motivation to play his approach shot with enthusiasm and confidence. In short, the difference between the par shooter and the bogey shooter often lies in a negative attitude toward the approach shot, which in turn comes from poor putting. In recent years, Arnold Palmer is a classic example of the erosion of putting confidence.

Middlecoff has spoken of the psychological value of being able to lay long approach putts dead to the pin for tap-ins—a knack which, he observed, could be attained only through practice and an adherence to sound putting principles.

"Those longish second putts," Cary said, "take a lot out of you even when you make 'em. When you keep having to make three- and four-foot putts to two-putt a green, it's going to wear you down eventually. You are going to find yourself a shaken and jumpy man as you walk to the next tee."

A classic, and, in some respects, tragic case revealing the

9

futility of trying to win while not putting well is Ben Hogan's. In his early sixties, Hogan is still a paragon of shotmakers. Reliable observers who have watched him play for years declare that Hogan almost never makes a really bad shot from tee to green. In fact, he comes closer to the ideal of hitting every green in the regulation number of strokes than any other player. Yet he never was able to win a tournament in which he putted badly, as invariably he did throughout the decade that began around the mid-1950's. Before then, when he putted well, or just fairly well, he was a consistent winner.

A locker room conversation between Jack Burke Jr. and Hogan, following a round in the 1965 Masters tournament, clearly indicated that both realized the serious effect poor putting was having on Hogan's game. When Hogan said he had carded a 73 on the round, Burke observed that 73 was an excellent score considering the difficulty Hogan was having sinking four-foot putts. Hogan agreed.

As it turned out, Hogan's 73 represented 35 shots to the greens (he hit the par-5 thirteenth in two and all the rest of the holes in regulation) plus 38 putts. This is not to say that Hogan was unaware of the value of good putting or did not work at this phase of the game. He was and did. But somehow the long years of competitive golf finally robbed him of the nerve control one needs on the greens.

The Hogan illustration emphasizes that even near-perfection from tee to green will not suffice unless backed up by at least fair putting.

One clear warning should be sounded before we go into details concerning the techniques used by many of golf's great putters. You should not be a conscious, slavish imitator of another golfer's putting style. Such putting masters as Deane Beman, Arnold Palmer, and Billy Casper, along with just about every other golfer who has spoken or written on the subject, have counseled specifically against one golfer's trying to make himself a carbon copy of another.

Palmer is a case in point. He stands to the putt knock-kneed, pigeon-toed, and altogether in what might be described as a hunched-up position. It is clear to the knowledgeable golfer that Palmer evolved his putting stance with a view to eliminating any possible body movement during the stroke. It worked for him. But

10

In putting, it is well to remember that the hole is more than two times wider than your golf ball. This relationship between the diameter of the hole (4-1/4 inches) and your golf ball (1.68 inches) allows a wide margin of error on all putts.

any other golfer might find the Palmer stance cramped and uncomfortable.

All putting authorities stress the importance of freedom and comfort in the stance. "Take a comfortable stance" is a piece of advice found in virtually every treatise on putting—usually quite early in the text, and frequently italicized. "Stand just as I do," on the other hand, is conspicuously absent. Yet while you should not try to mimic any of the great putters' stances exactly, you should emulate their efforts to find a putting stance that will provide a feeling of being firmly anchored in place and free from body movement during the putting stroke. (We shall see later that body movement, or sway, is one of the great enemies of effective putting.)

To carry our warning against excessive imitation further, consider the putting stance of Jack Nicklaus. Its distinctive feature is that Nicklaus' right shoulder is considerably lower than his left. This places the bulk of his weight on his right leg, and gives him the appearance of being sort of hunkered under the ball. Positioning most of one's weight on the right side goes against prevailing putting opinion, which calls for the weight to be either evenly distributed or mostly on the left side. But, as with Palmer, Nicklaus is guarding against the sway, and has found his own best way to do it.

11

As further illustration that even the most effective methods vary, Billy Casper advises, ''Have your weight equally distributed on both feet, or slightly on your left side,'' while George Low counsels, ''The weight should be slightly more on the left foot than on the right,'' This, he claims, seems to make it easier to hit the ball solidly and helps prevent swaying.

In respects other than stance, the experts differ in theory and practice. The point emphasized here is that the player who aspires to be a better putter should, while adhering to certain fundamentals, develop his own individual style. Let us put it this way:

The object of this book is to create a framework in which the instinct and natural skill of a player can find its own expression.

The book is divided into four parts. In part I you will read the individual methods and theories of the great putters. Part II sums up the principles of putting on which most of the great putters agree. Part III deals with specialized putting techniques such as lag putting, plumb-bobbing, side-saddle putting, the yips, reading greens, body putting, putting with your eye on the hole, and even takes a humorous look at what to do when everything else fails. In part IV you will learn how to get the most from your practice, why knowing the rules can save you strokes on the green and, finally, what you should look for when buying a putter.

# part I
# the great putters

# 1

# bobby jones

Robert Tyre Jones Jr., whom the golfing millions always knew as "Bobby" and his friends as "Bob," unquestionably was one of the greatest golfers of all time. Although he was an amateur player and never taught golf for a livelihood, he was a brilliant student of the swing. He wrote lucidly and prolifically on the subject and his essays on instruction have become over the years virtually a basic text, admired as much for their insight as for their elegance of style, a style as graceful as the author's golf swing.

Jones wrote this essay on putting in 1928. It remains one of the most perceptive single accounts of the subject ever written.

## on putting

□ comfort breeds steadiness
□ allow left arm to finish
□ work to hole short putts

The most difficult part of the game of golf is played on the putting green. Whatever may be the relative importance in the long run of the drive, the approach, and the putt, It Is certain that it is the putt which mars or finishes the job which the others have begun.

No man has yet been able to win a championship without putting well, taking advantage of his scoring opportunities by holing the putt after a fine iron shot, or saving precious strokes by sinking a

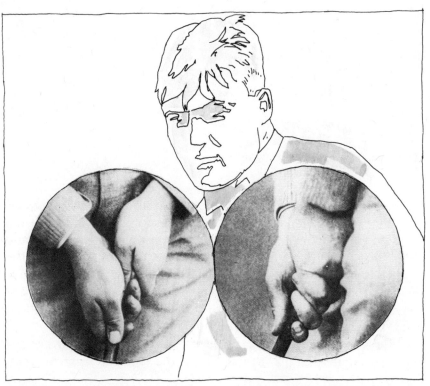

View of Bobby Jones' putting grip shows how Bobby opposed his wrists and hands and placed his thumbs straight down the shaft. He took the club back with the left hand and stroked with the right. The hands started the stroke touching the knickers.

good putt for a par after slack play in the other departments had caused him trouble.

One of the questions most frequently put to me is "What are the essential fundamentals of good putting?" It is a question over which I have pondered quite a lot. I have given more thought and attention to chipping and putting than to all other departments of the game combined, and I suppose it took me longer to acquire any proficiency there than in any of the others.

Form in golf varies greatly from day to day in every respect, from the driving on down, but I think it is harder to putt consistently well than it is to do anything else in the game.

It is impossible to prescribe any particular method which will assure good results. The matters of stance, grip, and the position of address should always be left to the player to work out for himself.

16

The main thing is to be comfortable, thoroughly relaxed, with no hint of strain. This is highly important. By attempting to duplicate another method, some players find themselves so cramped and strained that a smooth rhythmic stroke is impossible.

To hole a putt of any considerable length it is necessary to co-ordinate a number of factors. To find the exact line to the hole and to adjust the speed of the ball so that it will take every curve and roll with precision and curl into the cup, are things which human beings cannot accomplish with mathematical accuracy.

The very uncertainty attendant upon the success of even the well-hit putts should make us doubly anxious to learn to strike every one truly, for if we cannot be sure of the good ones how can we hope to sink the putts which we actually mis-hit with the clubhead?

There is much said about keeping the head and the body still, and taking the putter back with the left hand, and stroking with the right, all of which is very sound advice and helpful to the inexpert putter. But the majority of persons do well enough in these respects. Those who have played at all, quickly realize that they cannot permit the body to sway or move to any great extent, and most of them ap-preciate the difference between a smooth, flowing stroke and a stab or jab. That much, I think, is accepted and practiced with fair understanding.

I have noted, however, a very general tendency among certain putters, to confine the execution of the putting stroke exclusively to the wrists. Intent upon preserving a perfectly stationary head and body, the player swings the putter back and forth without taking up any of the motion with the arms, a strained, unnatural performance throughout.

In the first instance, if the arms are held firmly in position, and the arc of the stroke is gained entirely by the action of the wrists, it is impossible to provide a backswing of sufficient proportions for a putt of more than moderate length. If the distance to be traversed is great, it is then necessary to hit hard, with considerable effort and with consequent loss of rhythm. The putting stroke should always have the virtue of smoothness if it has no other.

A putt should always be hit along the ground, never lofted in the air. There again, the all-wrist stroke causes trouble, for, to com-plete the stroke without moving the arms, the clubhead must come up very sharply from the low point of the arc, and if this low point is reached before, or at impact, the ball must be lifted from the ground.

I believe every teacher will advise that the putterhead should finish low. Obviously, unless it stops at impact, it cannot finish low unless something is done to flatten the arc of the follow-through. And that can be accomplished only by allowing the left wrist and arm to move in a forward line as the ball is struck.

That I regard as the most necessary movement in the whole business of putting. And you see it omitted so many times. The omission results in what I call a "locked left wrist" and it may cause almost any sort of error. The remedy is a little more firmness in the left-hand grip as the ball is struck, and don't be afraid to let the arm move with the stroke and so remove itself from the way of the stroke.

It is a mistake to advise a person to keep his body still when putting. In making sure that the body will not move or turn there is a certain amount of rigidity set up which defeats the prime necessity — relaxation.

It is impossible to be quite still and at the same time relaxed, but it is not possible to hold one's self quite still and at the same time relax. The very thought of preventing motion causes stiffness. Whatever motion there is should be permitted rather than forced. This is my conception of perfect relaxation.

The first essential motion is that of the club. The easiest way to accomplish that without strain is by using the arms and hands. If the motion of the arms is sufficient to cause a movement at the body, then the body should move, and will move unless it sets up a resistance of its own.

I will agree that no body motion should be consciously and wilfully produced but if the putt requires a stroke long enough to suggest a movement of the hips or shoulders, it should not be resisted. The attitude of the player towards body motion should be entirely negative, and he may be conscious of it only after it has taken place. But he should never set himself against it. In the interests of timing and rhythm I believe it should be encouraged by a perfect willingness to move upon the slightest impulse.

The one great reason why most players find the long approach putts so difficult is that they refuse to employ the power of arms or body, and so either fail to produce enough force to reach the ob-

18

jective, or they force the stroke, just as they force a drive or an iron, and destroy the accuracy of it.

When the putt becomes merely another golf shot this trouble is removed. If the length is short only the wrists are needed. As the putt becomes longer the wrists must flex more and more, until a point is reached where it becomes more comfortable to move the arms as well.

I think the most important thing to be done on the putting green is to place the body in a comfortable position where it is perfectly balanced, yet free to move at the least suggestion of necessity. There should be perfect relaxation and no strain in any muscle. That done the putt is merely a matter of stroking the ball smoothly and easily toward the hole.

I do not like even to hear anything said about keeping the head or body still. It may be good practice but it is not a good thing to think about because the very effort invariably produces a rigidity which is not healthy. The more naturally one can fall into position the better off he will be.

One of Alex Smith's many dictums on golf has to do with putting — "The most important part of putting is getting the ball into the hole." At first glance this doesn't appear very enlightening but it isn't exactly as inane as it sounds. There are certainly many golfers who actually appear to lose sight of the first object of the game, and devote most of their attention to details of the stroke which, if left alone, would take care of themselves all right. Too much worrying about details of how the hitting is done is fatal to good putting. The stroke is of less importance in putting than in any other department of golf. At least, I am sure there is less cause for concern over the precise form in which it is made. Hence, a comfortable, easy position in hitting the ball is one fundamental requisite. It tends to steadiness in hitting, because a minimum of effort is needed, and it further eliminates any consideration of any special method or pose. Every time a thought is given to stance or stroke it is just so much taken away from the accomplishment of the one purpose of putting.

Probably because the objective is so very close in putting, there is an almost overwhelming temptation to lift the head in an effort to learn where the putt will stop before the ball has fairly started upon its way. Although after the ball is struck the damage, if

19

any, is done past repair, anxiety over the result often will not permit us to stroke the ball calmly in the proper manner.

The most common manifestation of looking up is a continual half-topping of approach putts. Struck with a swing ample for the distance if the ball is fairly hit, the half-top invariably leaves the ball short of the hole, often with a bothersome second putt to make.

A fine remedy is to be sure that the ball has been actually struck before looking up. That is by no means as hard to do in the case of a putt, as with a full shot from the fairway.

However, the range of the putt is so very important that to gaze fixedly at the ball for an appreciable length of time may be as bad as looking up. In no case must the player concentrate his attention upon the ball long enough for his visual measurement of distance to be disturbed.

All of which indicates that the first thing in putting to be considered is the slope and speed of the green. It is evident that no matter how accurately the ball may be struck, it is first necessary to select the line upon which it should be started.

As an indication that the line is the important thing, I can truthfully say that I have holed very few putts when I could not see definitely the path which the ball should follow into the hole. In any round there are always numbers of times when the proper line to the hole is obscure. If it were always visible we should miss few putts.

Working on this idea, it must appear that we should concern ourselves mainly with the more general contours of a slope rather than try to account for every little hop or roll which the ball is likely to take. This does not mean that we should be taking a haphazard shot at the hole, but only that we should determine upon a line which we want the ball to start, and hit firmly upon that line. Worrying about rough spots in the green has no effect except to make the stroke indecisive, and I believe that bad putting is due more to the effect which the green has upon the player than to that which it has upon the action of the ball.

There is one conception upon which I have always worked with fair success and which might furnish a useful hint to the reader. When putting across a side slope I try to make sure of keeping the ball above the hole so that it will always be falling towards the cup, the object being to make it tumble slowly into the upper side of the hole. If the speed is right, the putt cannot finish very far away.

20

The Jones putting stance. The ball is opposite the left toe. The heels have a mere half-inch between. The left eye is aligned on the ball. On the backswing the putterhead opens normally, but very slightly, owing to the opposed palms and wrists. Jones stroke was a "stroke," not a sharp hit, but it had a beautiful firmness. At the finish Jones comes through with little or no turnover; an effect of the opposed palms. The weight seems perfectly distributed on both feet.

The art of judging slope and speed is not entirely god-given. It is possible to a great degree to develop the faculty. But the major part of any putting practice should be directed to that end rather than to the development of a perfectly accurate stroke.

If day in and day out a man will concentrate upon hitting the ball on the line he thinks is the right one, and with a speed which he thinks is proper, and if he will let the luck and breaks take care of themselves, he will soon find that he is a much-improved putter. Many times long putts find the bottom of the hole but the man who thinks he can hole them consistently is much mistaken. It is the putt of three yards and less which really counts. Let a player acquire sufficient precision to hole the short putts with regularity and he can afford to take the long ones as they come.

The real test of a good putter is reliability. Not unfailing consistency, for everyone must have his lapses, and not absolute precision with the two and three yarders — but a consistency within human limits which rolls the long ones up close to the hole and rarely slips one of a yard or less.

To miss a putt of two, three, or even four feet seems about the most useless thing in the world. The texture of most of our greens upon which competitions are played is such that no valid excuse is offered the player. In almost every case, one may have the assurance that if struck properly the ball will find the cup.

The greatest difficulty in the short putt arises out of the fact that if we allow for the roll of the green, the stroke must be so delicate and the blow so gentle because of the meager space to be traversed. To strike a crisp and firm, and at the same time gentle blow, requires the very ultimate degree of what we call touch, and firm hitting is the essence of good putting.

For the putter of less extreme delicacy there is always open the method of spanking the ball into the back of the cup. Indeed, where there is a bit of roll to the green, I think that is the best method. If we endeavor to borrow on a short putt, there is always the danger of an error in gauging the speed which will be sufficient to allow the ball to fall off below the hole, or if we have hit it too hard, to keep it from taking the fall until it has passed the cup.

While I favor a free, sweeping swing for putting at middle and long distances, I do not believe that this method is reliable for the shorter ranges. The sweeping stroke is primarily one of delicacy, and delicacy is not so much desired on the holing out putts as direction. I think the best method is to take a short grip on the club and get the head down a good deal closer to the ball. I should also grip the club a bit tighter and strike the ball with a firm left wrist. The first necessity in holing short putts is to keep the putter blade from turning away from the line.

There is no possibility of exaggerating the value of being able to hole all the short or missable putts. It isn't even necessary to hole the long ones if the little ones are certain. I can recall match after match and tournament after tournament which might have been saved by holing a few short putts. And I know that I am not the only one who must repent errors of this kind, for almost every runner-up has missed enough putts under six feet to make him the winner with strokes to spare if he had holed them all.

Here is a lesson which I learned many years ago, and which has made my putting infinitely better than before.

In 1921 I was beaten badly in the Amateur Championship by Francis Ouimet, and although I was thoroughly out-played throughout, I could have made a much better fight of it if my putter had not refused to work. I was absolutely helpless on the greens during the whole tournament.

The day after Francis beat me I went over to Nassau, on Long Island, to see Jimmy Maiden, Stewart's brother. We were setting out to play as Jimmy emerged from his shop bearing a rusty old putter which he had christened "Calamity Jane."

"Now, Bobby," Jimmy said, "take this putter and hit the ball for the hole. Never mind about your stroke or your follow-through." And Jimmy showed me a method which he wanted me to adopt. He made me place the ball about opposite my right foot and strike sharply down upon it with the old goose-neck putter, the blade of the putter sticking into the ground and traveling not an inch past the ball. In other words, I was permitted no follow-through at all.

We started out to play, I following Jimmy's instructions to the letter. To make a long story short, I holed so many long putts on the first nine that it became a huge joke to everyone in the game. It became simply a matter of getting on the green and then down the ball would go. I was out in 31 and should have been better if I had played even decently up to the greens.

Of course, I didn't putt that way for very long, and the method suggested by Jimmy did not suit me exactly, but from it I gained one idea which was invaluable, namely, that following through upon the line of the putt has nothing to do with the result. Many putts are mis-hit or swung off line because the player attempts to guide the ball. We must make up our minds that nothing which happens to the club after the ball is struck makes the least bit of difference. When we pick out a line and hit the ball, we do it all. If we make a mistake that mistake remains. It is too late to correct it afterwards.

And while I am on the subject of the stroke, I should like to call attention to what I think is a mistaken idea. We have all heard the expression — "Never up, never in" — and — "Well, I gave that one

23

a chance, anyway" — used as excuses for over-running the hole, and many golfers feel that their duty is well done if, when confronted with an important putt, they hit the ball wildly past the cup. They don't stop to think that for a ball going fast the hole is really only an inch wide — that is, the very center of the hole must be hit — while, if the speed is right, the ball may go in the front, back or sides. Suffer the ignominy of being short if you must, but try to roll the ball just up to the cup. Many of them that are not precisely on line will drop, and in any event, the next one won't be so hard.

Just to show that even the best putters miss the little ones occasionally, I can give two illustrations by Walter Hagen, whom I regard as the most deadly and effective putter in competition that the game has ever seen. Hagen at Skokie in the second round, after gaining a big lead with a brilliant sixty-seven in the morning, lost no less than six strokes to par on the first two holes, mainly through putting lapses. The last one he missed on the tenth could not have been over eighteen inches. Again at Worcester I saw him take four putts on the fourteenth from a distance of less than twenty feet.

I am not writing this to cast reflections upon Hagen's artistry with the putter. I think that nothing any one could say would by one whit lessen his well-deserved reputation. But I want to emphasize the point that if these things can happen to the best, it behooves us of lesser ability to exercise care and caution.

In the final analysis there is little room for entertaining the hope that putting may be reduced to a science. Good putting is at best a fleeting blessing. Here today, gone tomorrow. It is not likely that anyone will ever attain so close to perfection that he will be able to hole out from fifteen to twenty feet with reasonable certainty. So I think we waste time and energy in trying to perfect a putting stroke which will be as accurate and as certain as that of a steam engine piston. There are too many other things which have to be right and every one is susceptible to human error.

# 2
# billy casper

For most of his career, Billy Casper has been known as a phenomenal putter. This sometimes rankles Casper, who is one of the game's most accomplished players and expert shotmakers. For a decade beginning in 1959, no one in the world played big-time tournament golf on so consistently high a level as Casper. Five times he won the Vardon Trophy, given to the professional golfer who records the lowest stroke average of the year. Twice he won the U.S. Open and once the Masters.

But the fact is that his fellow pros stand in awe of his putting. He is probably the outstanding exponent of the style known as "wrist" or "tap" putting. In this chapter, Casper describes the method and explains how and why he evolved it.

## tap putting

☐ all putting is 'feel'
☐ wrist action encourages a still body
☐ left hand guides the stroke

If you gave me only one word to describe putting, I would say, "Feel."

Sometimes when I putt my left foot is toed in . . . sometimes it's not. One time my stance may be open, another time closed a little. There's no reason for any of this. It's just a matter of what feels good to me at the time.

You must follow some basic principles to putt well (I don't

25

 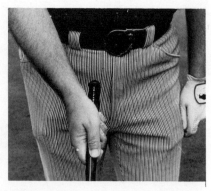

Casper uses a reverse overlap grip in putting, placing his right hand on the club first. The puttershaft runs from the base of the pad on his right hand to the first joint of his right forefinger. When he closes his right hand, the thumb rests on top of the

happen to think stance is one of them, by the way), but within the framework of these fundamentals I think you should find something that feels good to you. If something — a quirk in your stance or body position — works for you, then use it. If it doesn't work, try something else. That's the way I putt. It's the way I teach golf.

My objective in putting is to hit the back of the ball squarely, precisely at the bottom of the putting stroke. This makes the ball roll smoothly with overspin.

When I first began to play, I found the best way to achieve consistent, end-over-end roll was to keep my body still and let my wrists hinge back and forth, allowing the putterhead to swing freely through the ball. That's why my style of putting is sometimes referred to as "wrist" putting. Some people call it "tap" putting because of the tapping sensation one gets when the ball is struck.

Another equally important reason for using this style was that it allowed me to capitalize on the natural sensitivity and "feel" that is so essential to good putting.

The problem is that feel and touch are such inexact things. So much enters into it . . . how much rest you get, for example. If something you eat doesn't agree with you, I think it affects your feel and touch.

Feel is an indefinable something that you either have or you don't have on a given day, and controlling it is a problem. I've had my good times. When I won the 1959 U.S. Open at Winged Foot, I needed only 114 putts for 72 holes. In 1966, when I won the

shaft, pointing straight down. Casper's palms are in a facing position and square to his intended line. He carries the club more in the fingers of his left hand than many players, which allows greater feel and sensitivity.

Open at Olympic, I needed just 117, then 31 more in the playoff with Arnold Palmer. But I've also had bad streaks when I couldn't figure out where that feel went or how to get it back.

I do know you can develop feel through practice. The more you can get the putter in your hand, the more time you can spend stroking the ball, the better your feel and touch will be developed.

This is a natural law. We're creatures of habit. The more we do something, the more we become accustomed to it and so the better we are at it. I think you should spend twice as much time practicing short putts as you do the others, because you'll have twice as many of them.

Now, about those putting fundamentals. A still head and body position, a smooth, unhurried stroke, the blade kept square to the intended line . . . these are the basics which I believe must be employed to putt well.

The position of my hands on the club is pretty standard, if there is a standard in something as individualistic as putting. I do think the palms of your hands have to be pretty much in a facing position and square to the intended line of putt. Mine are, with the thumbs placed fairly straight up and down on the shaft.

I carry the club more in the fingers of the left hand than a lot of players do. This means the putter handle rests under the heel pad of the left hand. I can feel great sensitivity for the putterhead in my fingers. There is no sensation in the palms.

I choke down on the putter about half to three-quarters of an

27

Casper's tapping stroke is generated by the arms and wrists. His body is motionless. He allows the hinging action of the wrists to swing the putterhead back and forth along the chosen line.

inch for better control . . . and better feel.

As I said earlier, I don't think a square stance is particularly important. But aligning your body square to the line is important, as is an even weight distribution. Both of these encourage a still body and head position. If anything, the weight should be slightly forward, toward the ball. Head position is even more important. Your eyes should be over the ball, directly over the target line.

The ball is played directly inside the left heel, as are all my shots. I never move it, even for breaking putts as some do, because I feel leaving it in one place keeps your stroke more constant.

My hands are positioned directly over the ball — neither ahead of nor behind it. The wrists are arched rather than flat, but there is no strain in them. My hands are kept rather close to the body, the left hand sometimes actually brushing against my pants. I think positioning the hands too far from the body creates waver and other extraneous movement in the swing, because the position is more awkward.

28

Wrist putters have a tendency to pick up the putter on the
backswing. To cure this, Casper often finishes the stroke with the
putterhead resting on the ground, as shown in the picture above. Note that his
putting blade is square to his intended line on this left-breaking putt.

My arms hang naturally; I bend comfortably at the waist so my
eyes are over the target line and there is a little flex in my knees. The
outsides of my feet are about shoulder-width apart.

From this position I try to take the club back square to the line
and bring it back through along the line with my left hand.

My left hand does the putting, just as it should dominate in all
golf shots. The left hand pushes the club back to initiate the backswing and pulls it through on the forward stroke. The right hand
supplies power and feel, but the left hand guides. Putting is line and
touch, not power. Just as in the full swing, the right hand does not
add power until you come into the ball.

The most important thing to remember here is to keep the back
of the left hand moving as you come into the back of the ball. The

29

left hand must never break down; the right hand should never cross over or pass the left. If that happens, I invariably mis-hit the putt. I feel that both hands hit, or tap the putt.

Although I'm known as a wrist putter, I really use a combination of wrists and arms. Pure wrist putting is for shorter putts of up to 20 feet, depending on the speed of the putting surface. The longer the putt, the more my arms enter into the stroke.

For the shorter putts, a tapping stroke is best. This causes the ball to more quickly develop overspin and roll better over uneven portions of the putting surface. On longer putts, I use a more flowing stroke, again for better touch and feel.

Here's a tip that helps me when my putting goes bad: I try to stroke with the shaft of the putter rather than the blade. When I think of moving the shaft through the ball, the balde will move properly.

Keeping the blade square is vital, I believe. Obviously, my putterhead will come up off the ground on the backswing more than an arm-shoulder putter, but I want to keep the blade on line. It appears to people that my putterface is hooded on the backswing, but it's not. The hinging action of my wrists swings the putter head back and forth along the intended line. Sometimes I have a tendency to pick up the putter on the backswing, a common fault with wrist putters. When this happens I concentrate on trying to keep the blade low, especially through the stroke. Often I finish with the blade resting on the ground.

My type of stroke probably requires more practice than the arm-and-shoulder swing which a lot of players employ. But I think it allows me to develop more feel, and as I've said, I think that's the secret to holing more putts.

My emphasis in stroking a putt is on speed, rather than on going boldly for the back of the cup. I think that once you've picked out the line and positioned yourself properly over the ball, you forget about the line and worry only about hitting it at the correct speed.

My thought is to stop the ball within a two-foot circle or closer. I don't really care whether it's short or long, but I want the next putt from within that circle. I feel I can make most of those.

My grip pressure remains constant and is the same with both hands. It should not be tight. Hold the putter comfortably with no conscious pressuring by either hand. You have to be totally relaxed

30

when you're stroking a putt. If you've got any tension at all, stop and walk away from it. Any time you get rigid, you're in trouble. Again, we're talking about promoting more feel.

I putt pretty quickly, and I think this helps avoid tension. Don't fool around. Get it over with in a hurry. It's less taxing to the nervous system.

Of course, you must think positively when you're preparing to putt. If you think negatively, forget it. You really must discipline yourself to think in this positive manner.

I don't visualize the ball rolling into the cup as some players do, although I'm sure that's effective mental imagery. After I've determined the line — and I like to think I've been around long enough to make an accurate reading — I just think about making a proper stroke, getting the ball launched right. Those first six inches are so important. If you don't strike the ball squarely and get it rolling properly in those first six inches, you're going to have a diffi-cult time making putts. So the best advice I can give you is to put a solid stroke on the ball and not worry about the rest.

Putting can be a joy or the worst kind of frustration. When things are going right, everything is easy. You never think about what you're doing. But when they aren't going right, you start analyzing and concentrating and working hard . . . and sometimes you work too hard and defeat your purpose. Then it's time to relax and find a way to recapture that feel.

# 3

# bob
# charles

New Zealander Bob Charles is the best left-handed golfer in the world. He is also, in the opinion of many of his fellow professionals, the finest putter in the game today, left-handed, right-handed, cross-handed, or whatever.

Most of the golfers he has beaten would agree that he isn't a great striker of the ball — until he unsheaths that inevitable center-shafted putter. Then, as Gary Player dolefully said after being out-putted by Charles in the Piccadilly World Play-Match final in 1968: "You just want to look the other way."

A reserved, self-contained man, Charles slot putts day in, day out using a never-varying "pendulum" stroke on all sorts of greens all over the world. He does not regard putting as a matter of fluc-tuating fate or fortuitous inspiration, as do a lot of professionals. The talent that other people might regard as heaven-sent genius, he sees as being a product purely of technique and application.

Anybody can become and remain a very good putter, he says, if they work out a truly sound way to stroke the ball and then are pre-pared to practice enough to gain real confidence in that method.

# pendulum putting

☐ swing arms, hands like pendulum
☐ putter is extension of arms
☐ pendulum keeps blade on line

My conception of the soundest way to putt is that the arms and club swing exactly like a pendulum, at a very smooth, very even tempo, with the clubface square to the path of the stroke at every stage.

I often mentally visualize a pendulum action when I am putting, which helps me to make the stroke entirely with my arms, employing no wrist break or "give" in the hands whatsoever. I like to feel that my arms and the putter are a one-piece unit; that the putter swings simply because it is an extension of my arms. My arms actually pivot from my shoulders, but I like to feel that a point at the center of the back of my neck is the true pivotal point of the stroke.

If my putter shaft were perfectly upright at address, it could precisely reproduce the action of a pendulum and swing straight back and forth along the starting line of the putt. The putter shaft, however, extends upward toward me, which means that the head does not follow a straight-back, straight-through line. Its natural path of movement is inside the line on the backswing and inside it again on the follow-through, going straight along the line only at impact (the amount of this "inside" movement depends on the length of the swing, but is very slight with short putts). It should be emphasized that this inside-to-along-to-inside path is a purely mechanical result of making a pendulum-type swing with an implement offset from vertical, not a deliberate piece of manipulation by the golfer. If the swing is correctly made, the putter head will always be traveling squarely along the line at the moment of impact, which is all that really matters.

If you watch a true pendulum you will see that it gradually swings upward as it moves away from its lowest point. So does my putter. I make no effort to hold the club low to the ground either going back or stroking through the ball. I simply let it follow its natural pendulum-like rise and fall. However, if you compared me, an arm putter, with a wrist putter who also used the pendulum principle, my clubhead would appear to stay much closer to the

Charles demonstrates his putting technique, which he compares to the action of a pendulum. His wrists do not enter the stroke. Clubhead movement originates in his shoulders.

ground on both sides of the ball. This is due simply to the length of our respective pendulums: In my case the arms and club swing from my shoulders; in a wristy putter's case the club only swings from the wrists.

I use what is known as the reverse-overlap grip, probably the most popular of all methods of holding a putter because of the comfortable way it knits the hands together and enables them to operate and control the club in complete harmony.

In my completed grip, the backs of both my hands align exactly with the putter blade, and are thus "square" to the intended starting line of the putt as I address the ball. I place great emphasis on this "square" relationship of the hands to the putter face, both in my hold on the club and in the pendulum-type stroking action I employ.

To achieve maximum consistency I want to hold the club exactly the same way every time I putt. To reach that objective, and

34

Note how Charles' right shoulder lowers during backstroke, then swings up on throughstroke. Charles addresses putts with shaft almost perfectly vertical — the position he wants it to be in when the putterhead meets ball. He makes no special effort to keep putterhead low but achieves this effect by eliminating hinging of his wrists.

to promote "squareness" of alignment, all my putter grips have flat tops. This flattened surface is exactly at right angles to the putter blade, and I make a point of placing both thumbs upon it so that they lay flat and snug and point straight down the putter shaft. My putter grips are all correctly proportioned to the size of my hands, thus I can rely automatically on my thumb alignment as an overall positional checkpoint.

Touch, or "feel," in the hands is probably the most important single factor in putting. Unfortunately, it is also the most elusive. I understand from the scientists that "touch" must always be a variable factor, relating to one's daily metabolism, but in my ex-

Charles strives to keep backs of both hands aligned with putterhead and exactly square to intended starting line of putt. Placing both thumbs straight down the shaft helps him achieve this squareness consistently. He often varies width of his stance, but always positions himself at address so that eyes are centered directly above the back of ball, and toes, knees, hips and shoulders are parallel to starting line of putt.

perience it also has a lot to do with the pressures exerted by the hands and forearms in holding the club.

I am convinced that good stroking depends very much upon the hands working together, never even slightly in opposition to each other. Consequently I always try to hold the club with equal pressure in each hand, though the actual amount of pressure exerted is difficult to describe. If I hold it too loosely I lose control over the putter face and length of swing. If I squeeze it even a little, my sense of "feel" diminishes. I've had my best putting streaks when I seemed to be holding the club very lightly but also firmly.

I believe that in golf you should never needlessly place muscles in a state of stress, nor make unnecessary movements, but that you should give yourself as much freedom of action as possible. So my first priority in standing to a putt is comfort. The slightest tension or feeling of being out of balance tells me I will not stroke the ball correctly.

I like to have my weight evenly and solidly distributed between, and on, both feet — never rocking back on my heels or teetering on my toes. I lean over just far enough from the waist to sole the putter on the ground and bring my eyes directly over the ball. Club golfers commonly crouch too low, which produces tension in the legs and back, or they stand too erect in the body which forces the neck into a strained position.

I am not much concerned with the width of my stance, so long as I feel comfortable. Sometimes my feet are fairly close together, at other times well apart. I am much more concerned with the "square" alignment of my feet and body relative to the line along which I intend to start the ball rolling. Getting everything correctly squared up at this point eliminates the need to make compensations during the stroke. Square alignment reduces putting to its simplest, most consistent form.

To me, squareness at address means standing so that imaginary lines across my toes, knees, hips and shoulders all run parallel to the starting line of the putt I am about to play. I give great attention to this postural "squareness," especially to my feet, which I visually relate to the "line" of the putt in taking my address, and to my shoulders, the alignment of which, with my type of pendulum action, largely determines the path the putter will swing along.

Another important address factor, relating to my impression of "squareness," is ball location. Ideally I want to be so positioned that when I look down I want to see the club shaft exactly "square," not tilting forwards or backwards, positions which, if reproduced at impact, should change the clubface loft and alignment.

I am often asked what my eyes actually focus on when I am putting. The truth is I don't exactly know. Because of the importance of aligning the putter correctly at address, I suspect that I look at the blade of the club until the actual moment it begins to move back. After that my eyes seem to focus automatically on a point just behind the ball, and I try to keep them there until it is well on its way.

Tempo is extremely important in putting. In employing the pendulum principle, theoretically one should have the same momentum going back and coming forward with the club, but in practice this doesn't always work out. Hitting to the ball rather than through it — or "hitting and stopping," as some golfers call it — can easily lead to decelerating the clubhead before impact, the surest way I know to mis-hit putts. Thus, to ensure a solid hit, I try to swing the putter into the ball with just a little more momentum than I gave it going back. Also, for the same reason, I consciously strive to produce a follow-through at least equal in length to my backswing.

On putts up to about 30 feet on slow greens, and on fast greens up to about 40 feet, I try to maintain the momentum of stroke I've just described, controlling distance largely by the length of my backswing. This helps me swing the club at a consistent tempo, which I regard as an essential of good putting, on all putts I can reasonably hope to hole.

However, very long putts or very slow greens necessitate a modification of this technique. Faced with, say, a 50-footer on "wooly" Bermuda grass, I might find it difficult to control the very long backswing that my normal momentum of stroke would require. Particularly, there would be a danger of hand and body movement, which are prime causes of erratic putting.

Consequently with putts of this nature, instead of taking the putter back to a point where I might lose control over it, I take it back only about as far as I would for say a 30-foot putt on a medium-paced green, then increase the momentum of the club during the downswing sufficiently to hit the ball the required distance.

I do this more or less instinctively, measuring and creating the increased momentum through the "feel" in my hands. The technique requires experience, practice and confidence in one's basic stroke, but it usually will produce much better results, I believe, than a long, uncontrolled backswing.

I believe that good putting rests with the golfer and his method; I have no superstitious attachments to putters. Even if I had just won a tournament with one, I would change it if conditions the following week seemed to call for a different club.

If my stroke does not feel good, I will practice hard for up to 30 minutes a day — but never longer. Longer stints make me tired and

Charles feels the natural movement of the putterhead during the stroke is such that it will swing slightly inside the putt's line when it moves back from the ball, and then return to move along the line as it strikes the ball. Movement of clubhead to the inside is necessitated because the clubshaft sets into the head at an angle that is not 90 degrees. If it were, the natural clubhead path would be along the line throughout.

place too great a strain on my muscles. Also, I find it impossible to concentrate properly for more than 30 minutes. However, I do find "messing about" putting — playing around the green competitively with someone else — very good practice. I will do this for maybe an hour or so without getting tired or bored.

In practicing I don't concentrate on any particular length of putt. Though "feel" can only be developed by putting from varying distances, when I am working on my stroke, I'll usually putt from 15-20 feet.

The golfer who is trying to develop a good stroke needn't worry too much about where the ball finishes everytime. He should be chiefly concerned with the mechanics and tempo of his stroke, concentrating especially on making solid, square contact with the ball.

Once you have developed a good stroke, however, I think the most important concern in putting practice should be judging distance. This, really, is what putting is all about — the development of touch or "feel," the coordination of eye and hand. To achieve this, it is best to practice putts from varying distances, always trying to roll the ball at the right speed to take it just into the cup.

# 4
# deane beman

Deane Beman long has been regarded as one of golf's most knowledgeable players. His brilliant amateur record includes two U.S. Amateur championships, a British Amateur title and key roles on five Walker Cup teams. Even as an amateur his advice was sought by touring pros because of his keen analysis of the golf swing. Since turning pro in 1967, he has won five titles and over $400,000.

Beman is a relatively small man at 5-7 and is not long off the tee, but his reputation as a putter is large. Here Beman offers some fresh insights into putting in which he describes physical factors that govern what you can and cannot do with your putting stroke.

## banish putting conflicts

- ☐ hands instinctively square up at impact
- ☐ wrist putter can't keep blade low
- ☐ pendulum putters can't stand erect

The fact that I swing the club very differently than my long-time friend and rival, Jack Nicklaus, is proof that there is more than one way to play golf. Nevertheless, I believe there are some absolutes in the game that deal with crucial areas of the swing in which golfers most commonly make mistakes. Most professionals call them fundamentals, but I don't always agree with that term or the techniques which relate to it.

40

I prefer to call my absolutes "mutually exclusive" factors. This simply means that certain moves and positions in the swing or the putting stroke must be matched by other moves and positions. If they are, you can play well with your own particular style. But if your moves and positions do not match, if they are "mutually exclusive," your swing will be in conflict with itself and you will never play well consistently. It's not so much a matter of "correct" and "incorrect" as it is a matter of the factors in the swing relating to each other in harmony and in consistent fashion.

As a small man playing a power game, I have been obliged to study and experiment with golf more than most of my contemporaries on the professional tour. Here are some conclusions I have drawn from these studies, the major mutually exclusive factors that I believe are critical to a sound putting game, whatever a player's preferred method. They apply to you as much as to me or Jack.

If you have a "weak" or a "strong" putting grip, you can't return the putterface square to the target at impact. I believe that on every golf shot, from the drive through the putt, the hands instinctively return to a square position at impact. Swing at something, backhanded with your left hand and forehanded with your right, and you'll find you instinctively hit the target squarely.

The same thing happens in putting — the back of the left hand and the palm of the right naturally try to face the target at impact. Thus a golfer who grips his putter "weakly" — with his hands turned well to the left — will tend to return the putterface to the ball in an open position, or looking right of target. Conversely, a golfer with a "strong" grip — hands turned well to the right of the putter — will tend to return the putterface in a closed position, looking left of target, at impact.

This is why I believe that, whatever type of stroke is used, gripping the putter with the back of the left hand and the palm of the right square to the target line will most consistently return the face square at impact.

If you are a wrist putter, you can't keep the putterhead low. This is a matter of simple mechanics. Despite what you often hear, any kind of hinging of the wrists will lift the putterhead off the ground. It's the natural arc. Try it and see for yourself.

If his wrists have raised the putterhead, the golfer must drop or dip his left hand, arm and shoulder during the backswing to keep it low to the ground. Some tour professionals use this kind of action, but I believe it requires too many compensatory moves to be reliable over a period of time and prohibits making a repetitive stroke.

So, if you putt mainly with a hinging or breaking action of your wrists, allow the putterhead to come naturally off the ground in the

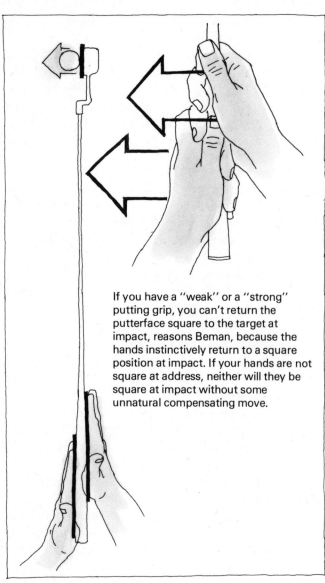

If you have a "weak" or a "strong" putting grip, you can't return the putterface square to the target at impact, reasons Beman, because the hands instinctively return to a square position at impact. If your hands are not square at address, neither will they be square at impact without some unnatural compensating move.

backswing, as Billy Casper does, and you'll putt more consistently.

If you address a putt with the ball well away from your body, you can't keep the path of the putter close to the target line. The arc of the putterhead should be kept as close as possible to your target for the sake of consistency. To do this, you should position the ball as close to your body at address as is comfortably possible. The farther you stand from the ball on any golf shot, the more acutely the clubhead will swing inside the target line on the backswing and after impact.

If you stand erect at address while putting with a shoulder stroke, you can't swing the putterface squarely back from and through the ball. Keeping the putterface as square as possible to the target line is basic to good putting, irrespective of the stroke used. I believe a stroking action emanating from the shoulders, with the

Wrist putters can't keep the putterhead low, Beman observes, because the hinging wrists lift the putterhead off the ground (right). Wrist putters who try compensatory moves like dipping the left shoulder (left) invite inconsistency.

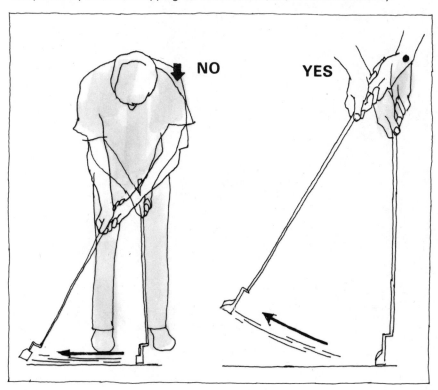

arms, wrists and hands locked into a solid unit, produces the least clubhead variance. In fact, although I now putt with a combination arm-and-wrist stroke, if I had it to do again, I'd change to a shoulder stroke, modeling myself after Bob Charles, the finest shoulder-stroker in golf.

If you use a shoulder stroke, your address posture has a big bearing on the "squareness" of your putterface during the stroke. If your upper body is erect at address, your shoulders must turn in a horizontal or level plane to swing the putter. If your arms, hands and club are solidly locked to your shoulders, the effect of this level turn will be to open the putterface while swinging the club inside the target line on the backswing. At impact and on the follow-through the clubhead will quickly swing back inside the target line and the

The farther you stand away from the ball at address, the farther inside you will swing the putterhead on the backswing. The reverse is also true—the closer you stand to the ball, the straighter back you can swing the putterhead naturally.

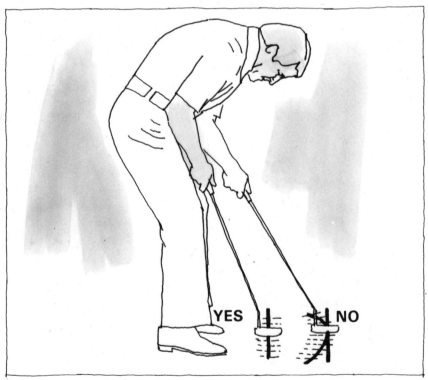

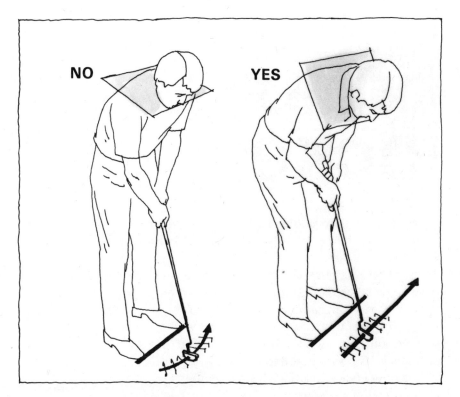

NO

YES

If you stand erect, you can't swing back the putterhead on a straight line, Beman explains, because the shoulders are level. Conversely, if you tilt the shoulders, you will be able to swing back the putterhead on a straighter line.

face will close. This opening and closing motion is almost unavoidable with a level shoulder turn, unless you compensate by manipulating the putter with your hands.

To keep the putterface as square to the target as possible throughout the stroke, the shoulder putter should lean his upper body forward from the waist, folding his arms into his body. His shoulders then can operate in a vertical or tilted plane that allows the putterhead to be swung nearly straight back from and straight through the ball, with the opening and closing of the face kept to a minimum.

# 5

# bobby locke

Many believe that Bobby Locke is the greatest putter who ever lived. His full name is Arthur D'Arcy Locke, and his beefy South African figure and lazy hooker's swing caused some amusement when it first was observed in the United States. He even hooked his putts. The snickering stopped abruptly when Locke began beating the top American stars of his day, including Hogan, Snead and Demaret. All of them agreed Locke was a phenomenal putter. What was his putting secret? He never hurried. He never changed his putter. His basic approach to putting was ritualistic and never varied. This is how Locke describes his technique.

## topspin puts it in

□ end-over-end roll is vital
□ feel putterhead in fingers
□ swing from inside the line

Very early in my career I realized that putting was half the game of golf. No matter how well I might play the long shots, if I could not putt I would never win. When I came to play championship golf, I was a good enough putter to set myself a target. To me, 32 putts represented a fair round, 30 putts a good round, and 28 putts a very good round. And I had a lot of 28-putt rounds.

My first objective in putting has always been to impart topspin to the ball. By that I mean causing the ball to roll immediately as truly end-over-end as possible—without any skidding, sidespinning or hopping.

There are two reasons why I consider this pure topspin action vitally important to good putting:

First, the player who consistently can produce such a roll usually develops the best sense of distance; the regularity of the ball's movement enables him to gauge the speed of his putts very precisely, day in and day out.

Second, a ball rolling truly end-over-end, if it isn't traveling too fast, will often fall into the hole from the "side door," whereas a ball rolling eccentrically often will spin out if it hits the side of the hole. Thus, true roll gives the player four entrances to the hole—the front of the cup if his putt is "dying"; the back of the cup if the putt is going a little too fast but is on line and either side of the cup if the putt is the right strength but marginally off line.

My second objective in the days when I was trying to develop a good putting stroke was to make it as similar as possible to the way I played all my other shots. From a young age I recognized the importance of consistency, or repeatability, in golf. The fewer variations in one's technique, the more consistent one becomes.

It might be most helpful, in describing my putting philosophy and method, to look at the various facets separately:

Most putts are missed not because they are mis-hit, but because the golfer has started the ball in either the wrong direction or at the wrong speed or both. Thus, I cannot overstress how vital it is to read every putt accurately before you actually stroke it.

My first concern in looking over a putt is the ball's speed. I first examine the line of the putt generally to get an overall impression of how hard I should stroke the ball. In so doing I concentrate particularly on a radius of about four feet around the hole. Here, as the ball ends its journey, is where every putt will be made or marred. I give very special attention to the type and length of the grass and to the contours in the immediate vicinity of the hole, gradually pulling together in my mind a clear picture of overall pace.

I have a basic rule of thumb for greens of differing pace. On a fast green I aim to hit the ball six inches short of the actual hole; on medium-paced greens I putt to drop the ball just over the front lip of the hole; on slow greens I putt firmly for the back of the cup.

47

Once I have a clear idea of pace and how the ball will break around the hole, I return to a position behind the ball to examine the starting line of the putt. My major concerns now are the hills and hollows between the ball and the four-foot radius around the cup. Having carefully assessed these, I marry the picture I get of ground contour to the picture I already have of the speed of the putt, until I form a clear mind's-eye view of the ball running across the green and into the hole.

Once I have made up my mind about the line and speed, I never change it. Second guesses are fatal in putting. Make up your mind and stick to your decision.

It seems to me relatively unimportant what kind of putter you use, so long as it is your friend. I found a putter I liked early in my career and I stuck with it because it almost always was my friend. This putter is hickory-shafted with a long, narrow blade and a leather grip. The only unusual thing about it is that it is a good deal longer than standard. I found that the extra length gives me a better "head feel" so that I can more easily sense and control the weight of the clubhead as I swing.

I always grip the putter at the very end of the shaft, and I never change the position of my hands on the club, whatever the type or length of putt. That would breed inconsistency.

The art of putting lies in the fingertips. You are fortunate indeed if you have a delicate touch. If you don't, you will have to work hard to avoid gripping the putter too tightly. Consistently good putting— rather than sporadically good putting—is impossible, I believe, with a tight grip.

My grip on the putter is the same overlapping grip I use for all my shots, with the one modification that I place both my thumbs down the top of the shaft. This helps me produce a stroke that imparts true topspin to the ball. Equally important, it helps me swing the putterhead back without opening the face and return it through the ball dead on line to my target.

At address I distribute my weight evenly and comfortably between my feet to protect my balance. My feet are about three inches apart, with the right foot drawn about three inches back behind my left foot to give me what is known as a closed stance. I adopted the closed stance a long time ago because it helped me avoid cutting across the ball from outside the line, which would have imparted

48

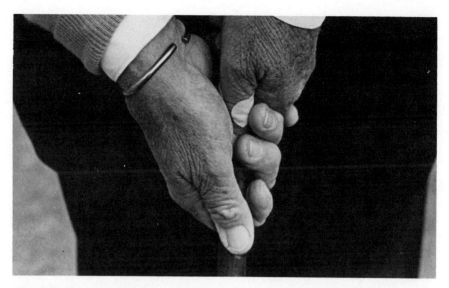

Bobby Locke putts with same Vardon grip he uses on full shots. Thumbs are placed down the top of the shaft. Grip is lightly held in the fingers. He grips the putter at the very end of the shaft.

sidespin to it. I use a similar stance on other shots for the same reason.

I position the ball relative to my feet in the same place on every putt — opposite my left toe. I know that some accomplished players change the position of the ball relative to the break of the putt, but I believe that in my case this would breed inconsistency.

The reason for positioning the ball opposite my left toe is that from here I am able to strike it slightly on the upswing, just after the putterhead has reached the bottom of its arc. This greatly helps me to impart true topspin to the ball. If the ball were farther back, I might have a tendency to chop down on it and impart backspin or sidespin.

At address I also position the ball opposite the toe of my putter, but I actually strike my putts on the center of the blade. I do this as further insurance against cutting across the ball from outside the line. This may seem unusual, but the fact is that if one addresses the ball opposite the center of the blade, there is a tendency to swing outside the line on the backswing, resulting in a cutting action at impact. Try it for yourself and see.

Addressing the ball opposite the toe of the putter blade also

Locke's stance is closed, to guard against cutting across the ball, and narrow. The ball is addressed near toe of the blade as further insurance against swinging outside on backswing and slicing putt. Locke takes the putter back distinctly inside and with a slightly hooded face because he wants to impart topspin to the ball. He shuns wrist movement because he believes it breeds inconsistency.

seems to make it easier to take the club back inside the line of the putt. This is an absolute cornerstone of my method; I have never found any way of applying true topspin to the ball without swinging the putterhead from inside the line.

In taking the putter back distinctly inside, I also endeavor to keep it as low to the ground as possible, almost brushing the grass, to avoid any downward chopping of the ball. More important is keeping the blade square to the starting line of the putt, or even closing it a little during the backswing. This is known as "hooding" the face and is a very important part of my stroke. Walter Hagen proved to me in 1937 that this type of backswing was the only one that would impart true topspin to the ball, and I am very happy that I listened to him and copied his method.

There is no wristwork in my backswing. Wristwork in putting also breeds inconsistency. However, one thing that does result from hooding the face is that my left wrist turns slightly "under" on the backswing. The longer the stroke, the more the back of my left hand points toward the grass.

To most observers, it appears that at the completion of my backswing the putterface is slightly closed. It may well be, but to me — as it should be to you — the feeling is that it is still square to the starting line of the putt. So long as it isn't open to that line, I am not too concerned.

I have always thought of the ideal putter swing as matching that of a clock's pendulum, slow and very smooth, with the clubhead going through the same distance it goes back. It's a very simple repetitive movement and a fine mental picture to have in your mind.

Thus, in returning the putter to the ball, I try to swing it very smoothly at the same pace I swung it back. Again, there is no wrist action. The putter is swung by my hands, wrists and arms as a unit; my left wrist at impact has exactly the same relationship to my left arm that it had at address. This insures that the putter blade remains square to my target through impact and well into the follow-through.

A vitally important point, especially on the through-swing, is keeping your head down and still. Look at the ball's original position until the ball itself vanishes from sight. If your head moves, everything is for naught. My head eventually turns to let me watch what is happening to the ball, but it swivels and never sways forward.

I still have my good days on the greens. I think, if you give my method a try, you will too.

# 6
# george low

George Low often is called the greatest putter in the world, by other experts in addition to himself. He was a good enough tour player years ago to be low pro when amateur Freddie Haas ended Byron Nelson's record victory streak at Memphis in 1945, but his reputation really has been built since he retired, mainly in money matches before small galleries of knowing insiders.

"George gets around more than anybody else I know," says his old friend Jimmy Demaret, no sit-at-home either, "and he has made a science out of putting. I guess George has putted every green in the world."

The stories about the heavyset Low's putting exploits are told long into the night during big tournaments. Leo Fraser, former president of the PGA, cannot recall Low ever ducking a challenge. "One of his favorite tricks," says Fraser, "is using the instep of his right foot for a putter. He can kill you from five feet that way." Low, crafty as well as talented, has been known to doctor up an umbrella like a putter and win with it. Doug Sanders says Low can putt better with a wedge than most people can with a putter.

"I have to admit I'm probably the best putter in the world," Low modestly says, "probably because I was born with a great feel and because I have practiced putting more than anyone else. When I was in my late 20s I went back to Scotland with my father, a golf professional who was from there, and I broke my back. We were at Carnoustie, which had a 36-hole putting clock, and once I could get up and around there was nothing else to do but putt. I would putt all day long. I've been beaten, but never over the long haul."

One of Low's favorite recollections is of a putting-green show-down with Ky Laffoon at Pinehurst No. 2. "We went at it from morning till evening, playing to 21," he says. "You got two points for holing a putt, four points for holing a putt on top of a holed putt, one point for nearest to the hole. I had him until it got dark, but we kept playing and he got even. I couldn't beat that Indian — he could see at night."

The consensus among today's touring pros is that Low, 60 now, has lost some of his renowned putting eye and touch but is the best teacher of putting in the game. He has given lessons, usually solicited, to most of the top putters, including Jack Nicklaus and Arnold Palmer.

Low has always been rather mysterious about his method, occasionally letting drop an insight into his theories but until now never disclosing his system in full. In the following exclusive article he gives the keys he believes can make a better putter out of anyone. "You can teach feel only up to a point," he says, "but good mechanics promote good feel. I believe anybody can understand the points I'm making. If somebody tries my method and isn't satisfied, I'll be glad to give him a chance to get his money back in a little putting match."

# secrets of world's greatest putter

☐ feel with your thumbs
☐ put weight on left heel
☐ stroke like a swinging gate

Everything I am going to say about putting is based on one objective — to develop a repeating stroke. For me it all starts with the thumbs. You feel with your thumbs.

If you don't believe me, try this experiment. Reach into your pocket and pick out a coin. You're feeling the coin essentially with your thumb, right? The thumb is the last thing to pinch the coin and the most sensitive part of your hand. Therefore we want to maximize the role of the thumbs in putting.

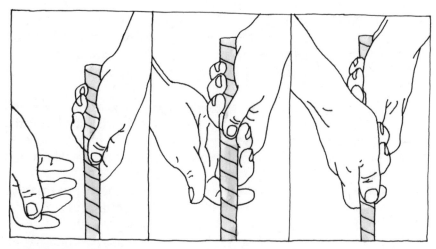

George Low says the key to putting is feeling with the thumbs, and thus his putting grip shows both thumbs on top of the putter. Low says a "short" thumb position — with only the first joint touching the putter handle — produces more feel than a "long" thumb position where the thumb is extended flat along the handle. He holds the putter at the top of the grip on putts of all lengths because he believes this gives him the same feel on every putt.

There are many effective ways of gripping a putter, but whatever grip you employ I believe you must have both thumbs on top of the putter for better feel. Once you have your thumbs pointing down the top of the shaft, pull them up short to get more feel. Experiment and you'll convince yourself that a long thumb gives you less feel than a short thumb. Also, with short thumbs you will be able to take the putter back inside the line more consistently, another key I will discuss later.

Naturally a flat-topped putter grip is going to be easier to handle with the thumbs on top. I hold the putter at the top of the grip on all putts, from two feet or 62 feet. I see a lot of players choking down on the putter, especially on little putts, but when you do that you aren't going to get the same feel every time. You are working with a different club — with a different swingweight. Again, the whole idea is to develop a stroke that will repeat time after time, and that means cutting out as many variables as possible.

I change my grip pressure depending on the type of putt, and I change it through my thumbs. I grip more lightly on fast greens or downhill putts, for a quieter stroke. I take a tighter grip on slow greens when I have to give the ball a harder rap. I grip tighter on short putts too, to beat the tendency to ease up through the ball and not be firm enough.

I liken changing my grip pressure to playing different musical instruments. Hitting a fast downhill putt is akin to playing a violin. You never see a good violinist sawing his bow across the strings. He makes a looser, flowing motion. A man playing a bass fiddle, on the other hand, is like a man putting on a slow green. He makes more of a sawing motion.

The secret is that I add or subtract grip pressure through my thumbs. I feel with my thumbs. I want to get the feeling I'm hitting the ball with my thumbs.

You should be as still as possible when putting. To keep from moving I put my weight on my left heel. That anchors me as solidly as if I were encased in a block of cement.

Bob Charles is a great example of a man who is all but motionless when he putts. He and all the other great putters operate mainly from the elbows down. The rest of the body is motionless, particularly the head. If the head moves, the blade of the putter is going to be affected . . . adversely.

When I tell you to focus your weight on your left heel, I don't mean to tilt your body. I told one weekend player to put his weight on his left heel and he immediately did a remarkable imitation of the Leaning Tower of Pisa. He was almost falling toward the hole. Just concentrate on having your weight on your left heel.

Stand up and try it. Put your weight on your left heel. Can you sway now? Not very easily.

Getting your weight on your left heel goes along with having an open stance, another one of my requisites. My left foot is withdrawn slightly — and I do mean slightly — from the line of the putt on all putts. If you overdo it you'll be hitting your right foot with the putter, but a slightly open stance has several advantages.

For one thing, it's easier to put your weight on your left heel. For another, it's an uncramped position. You're more comfortable — and comfort is vital in putting. For another thing, your vision is better. You can see from behind the ball to the hole with no distortion and visualize the line much more clearly.

With a square stance you're also prone to push-block the putt to the right. But with an open stance you are in better position to bring the putter through the ball squarely, because your left side is out of the way.

My stance is open to the target line to the same degree on breaking putts as on straight putts. I see thousands of average players who are weak on breaking putts because they don't adjust their stance to the line. You have to set up to the line, not the cup. Then you make the same stroke you would make for a straight putt. If you don't adjust your stance on a 30-foot putt that is going to break from right to left, for example, you'll probably push the putt badly. The more the break, the more the adjustment.

The main point I am making is that my feet are open to the line of the putt the same amount on a straight putt or a breaking putt, and my stroke never changes. Once you adjust your feet, every putt becomes a straight putt.

I line up the ball in the same spot every time: off the inside of the ball of my left foot. I make sure that my left index finger — the one that is interlocked — is just ahead of the ball at address. That all but guarantees me an accelerating stroke through the ball and solid contact. My hands are in close to my body so that I can make a flat, natural stroke.

Like everything else I'm saying, this is the way I putt and you may want to make adjustments to suit your individual case.

When you take a stroke with your putter, the head of the club travels in a swinging arc. Be sure the face is always squared to this arc. Then you will return the face to the ball in the same position it was in when you started your stroke.

It's like opening and shutting a gate. A gate always swings back into its original position. As the gate opens and shuts, it is continually squared to its swinging arc. You should stroke putts with a similar swinging arc. Think of your putterhead as being a gate opening and closing.

Like a gate, the putter comes back inside the line of the putt and then returns to a square position at impact. The putter should not, as so many people advise, come straight back on the line of the putt — not unless you are dealing with a very short putt. It starts back straight but then follows its natural tendency to come inside the line, just as a full swing with a driver comes inside. A putt is a miniature golf swing.

To be sure I take the putter inside on the backstroke, I line up

Low uses a slightly open putting stance for comfort and better visual sighting to the hole. This also makes it easier for him to focus his weight on the left heel, which anchors him solidly and helps prevent swaying. The open stance puts him in better position to swing the putter through the ball on line, because his left side is out of the way. To ensure that his backswing is distinctly inside, Low addresses the ball in the heel of the club.

the ball off the heel of the club. I'm not actually going to hit the ball off the neck of the putter, but by addressing the ball there I avoid the common tendency to take the putter back outside the line. I hit the ball in the center of the putterface better by addressing it off the heel. Try it and see if you don't get solider contact.

When we talk about bringing the putter back inside the line, we are not speaking of hooding the face — taking loft off it. Too many people bring the putter back inside but hood it and get all sorts of disastrous results.

How far do you take the putterhead back? I have no formula. I've often heard it said that most people take it back too far and then quit on the throughstroke. I disagree. The reason many people quit on the stroke is that they address the ball poorly, or sway, or fail to keep the left wrist going through the ball — not because they take the putter back too far. If you make a short, jabbing stroke you won't have good rhythm, and rhythm is as important to putting as it is to Nureyev's dancing. I prefer a longer backstroke that lets the putterhead do the work.

I also suggest a slight pause, a fraction of a second, between the completion of the backswing and the start of the forward stroke. You'd be surprised how much your tempo and rhythm, and thus feel and touch, improve when you do this.

Nerves will have a lot to do with how far back you can take the putter. If your nerves are good, you can take it back farther. When I'm under extra pressure I'll shorten and firm up my stroke.

The other factor in determining how far back to take the putter is the weight of the putterhead. Your mind can compute the distance. Take the putter back as far as the weight of the head demands to bring it through and get the ball in the hole. And take it back slowly.

When I say to hit a putt, I mean to hit it. You hit a putt the same as you hit any other golf shot. You don't baby it. I see people doing everything to a putt except hitting it, and I know they'll never be consistently effective. Many of them try to shove the ball, and they spin it to the right almost every time. Don't be afraid to give a putt a hit, even a delicate four-footer. Imagine that the ball has a tack in the back and you want to drive the tack in. You'd give it a solid rap, right?

I could go on for a week about putting, but if you work with more than three or four main thoughts you'll do yourself more harm than good by confusing yourself. Concentrate on feeling with your thumbs, getting your weight on your left heel, and swinging like a gate, and see if you don't putt better right away. In a couple of weeks you might be coming around to challenge me.

# 7
# jack nicklaus

If Jack Nicklaus were not so sensational on his longer shots, he probably would carry the reputation of "world's greatest putter" on his back. That is the opinion of Byron Nelson who has been a keen observer of Nicklaus' career. Nelson, himself an "immortal," says he has lost count of the times he has perched on a television tower beside the 18th green, where he regularly commentates big tournaments for ABC-TV, watching as Nicklaus rolled in a pressure-laden putt.

"Looking back," Nelson says, "I realize how underrated this man from Ohio is as a putter." Nelson, a member of the Golf Digest professional panel, analyzes the Nicklaus putting method and explains why it is so successful.

## byron nelson explains jack's method

□ set up behind ball
□ keep head and body still
□ stroke decisively

When you think of Jack Nicklaus, you immediately conjure up thoughts of a smashing drive flying 300 yards and rolling dead a country mile ahead of shots hit by his playing companions. You also think of his marvelous strength from the rough that allows him to maintain clubhead speed and reach the putting surface from depths

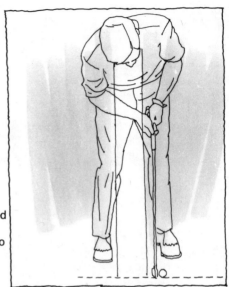

Jack Nicklaus says he has always putted best with a feeling that he is set up behind the ball. This setup allows him to look "through" the ball toward the target and hit the ball following his chosen line.

that are impossible for almost any other player. These are credits well deserved by this champion of more major events than any golfer in history. But no one should overlook his putting . . . he's a master on the short grass. I know if I had a 15-footer to win or tie a tournament, I don't know of any fellow I'd rather have strike it for me than Jack.

Let's take a look at Nicklaus the putter. Since putting is very much an individual, suit-yourself thing, his method differs greatly from most other recognized super-putters. He looks different than Arnold Palmer or George Archer and, most certainly, than Sam Snead on the greens. But the basic objectives are the same, no matter who is holding the putter. You must do an adequate "read" of the green, must apply an efficient stroke and must execute with confidence.

Nicklaus sets himself up behind the ball, bending at the angle so he can often see both the ball and the cup without moving his head. He addresses the ball opposite his left toe and appears to be looking at the intended line of the putt from behind the ball instead of beside it. "I've always putted best with a feeling that I am set up behind the ball, hitting it away from me," Jack says. "Set up like this, I can look 'through' the ball to my target. This optical angle is critical to my rolling the ball smoothly and squarely forward along

60

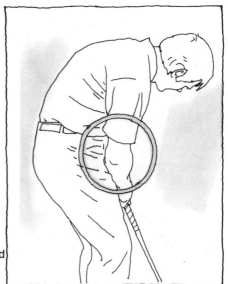

Nicklaus keeps his right elbow snugly against his right side while putting, to guard against closing the putterface and also to avoid swinging outside the intended line of his putt.

the precise line I have chosen.''

The right elbow is kept snug against Jack's side, a guard against closing the clubface of the putter during his stroke. This method also seems to aid him in keeping his body—and most importantly his head—completely still during the stroke. I don't think Nicklaus could tuck his elbow like that if he moved his right hand more on top of the putter. He instead keeps the hand on the ''strong'' side, behind the putter as it moves toward the target. That makes it much more simple to keep the elbow hugging his right side.

When Nicklaus has a streak of poor putting, he claims that his left shoulder unconsciously lifts up a little. I'd have to agree with that. He even seems to be lifting his head at times. ''Many poor putters do this without ever realizing it,'' Jack says. ''When this happens I concentrate on keeping my left shoulder 'low' throughout the stroke.'' But this doesn't happen too often. Jack has marvelous control of his body on any type of shot, but especially with the putter.

I'll tell you another little mannerism Nicklaus has while putting. Maybe he doesn't even realize it, but Jack will seemingly get all set to stroke the ball and then lift up to an almost straight position before re-setting for the shot. It seems as though he takes one last look, making sure he has read the green properly and that all is in order before trying to knock the ball into the cup.

Once Jack is completely set up over the ball, the putterhead is just slightly "behind" his hands. This is extremely important in making a smooth and effective stroke. Jack's hands always seem to be over the ball, which causes the shaft of his putter to stand at a slight angle when the putterhead is placed behind the ball. Just before he hits, Nicklaus seems to be looking at the ball with his right eye with his head cocked toward the target. Maybe he has some kind of cinemascopic vision that allows him to see the entire trail of a 25-foot putt, I don't know. "Looking directly down on the ball is vital for me, too," Nicklaus says. "If my eyes are out beyond the ball, I tend to pull putts left; if my eyes are inside the line, I tend to push putts right."

Now for the stroke itself. Nicklaus has done all his homework, all his surveying and mechanical aligning. But the true test comes when he makes impact.

Nicklaus starts the putterhead back almost exactly straight from the ball, keeping the blade square to the target. Keeping his hands well ahead of the putterhead at all times seems to help. Also, the putterhead stays relatively low to the ground on both the backswing and throughswing. As impact approaches, the putterhead does not undergo any deceleration. It continues as a smooth, firm stroke. There is no "pop" of the ball at impact, as is advocated by some noted putters. This smooth, firm stroke is something I preach myself when advising people on putting since, if your timing gets off, a popping motion can really cause you problems. I think, as I'm certain Nicklaus does, that a smooth stroke through the ball is less likely to be bothered by problems in your timing.

One thing I've heard Jack say about his putting is that he actually holds his breath while stroking the ball. Don't laugh. He certainly isn't gasping because of fear of what's about to happen with the putt. It's just that this marvelous golf craftsman wants to eliminate all the possible problems in making any kind of swing at the ball. He says that the breath-holding trick prevents his diaphragm from moving, thus allowing him to remain as still as humanly possible just as the stroke is executed.

Nicklaus, unlike some top professionals, never seems to make a "cut" shot on a putt—slicing across the ball from outside the line to inside. He is more like a piston, going straight back and then straight

Nicklaus sets up with his eyes directly over the line of the putt, and keeps this eye-to-ball-to-hole relationship throughout his putting stroke. If his eyes are beyond the line, he tends to pull putts left. If his eyes are inside the line, he tends to push putts right.

through the ball. I think setting up with his weight apparently on the right foot helps him to push the ball toward its target. There seems to be less room for error in the Nicklaus Method.

Many putters, even some $100,000-a-year tour stars, have a real problem with getting too "wristy" in their putting stroke. I know Tommy Aaron, the 1973 Masters champion, has always said this, even though Tommy happens to be a pretty fair putter, especially from great distances. The problem is allowing the putterhead to flip past your hands before impact, or at impact. This tends to make you pull the putt to the left. Nicklaus is great at keeping the hands ahead of the putterhead, and seldom has difficulty with being too wristy. Of all the tips you read or hear about putting, this is one not to forget. It's a big, big item in becoming a standout on the putting green.

The most important factor for any putter other than basic skills, is being able to putt with confidence. Even a 100 shooter can get the feel that he's going to make every 10-footer and knock cross-country putts up within 18 inches of the hole. At other times, you might feel you couldn't knock a putt into a rainbarrel. I've felt that way a few times myself. I feel that this meticulous Nicklaus ap-

Intense concentration marks the Nicklaus putting method. Nelson believes Jack's meticulous approach to putting helps him putt with such confidence. He believes in his setup and his stroke, something all golfers should work to achieve.

proach to putting is something that helps him putt with such wonderful confidence. He seems to believe in every little movement, in his basic setup and in the stroke itself.

I almost never get the feeling that Nicklaus is thinking of anything but making a terrific attempt at putting the ball into the hole. Sure, when he's facing a 45-footer it's a bit different. Jack then is trying to get it close, attempting to roll it inside an imaginary circle with a three-foot radius. His goals with the putter are no different than those of a dozen or two other top professionals. The big difference is that Nicklaus does it with more consistency.

Another of the positive things about Nicklaus as a putter is his obvious command of what he's trying to accomplish. He never seems indecisive. This is obvious on the fairways, in the roughs and on the tees as well as on the green. He looks a situation over most carefully, makes his mind up and then grabs a stick from his bag. How many times have you seen him take a club and then exchange it for another? Not very often, if ever. This confidence in his ability is magnified on the green. Nicklaus knows, as any golfer does, that he

# 3
# george archer

Most of his fellow-professionals say that if they had a putt of eight feet or less that absolutely had to be made, the man they would choose to make it is George Archer. His reputation for holing pressure putts spans a career that began in 1964 and includes one Masters title, 11 tour victories and earnings of over $800,000.

Archer's ability with the putting blade is remarkable in view of his gangly, 6-6 frame. Most outstanding putters are built much closer to the ground. George has the ability few tall men can muster for keeping his body still, a technique he discusses in this chapter.

Archer would not advocate that everyone putt like he does. "I'd say give my method a try, and if it works as well for you as it does for me, then we're both happy," Archer states. "If it doesn't work, look around for something else. But once you've found a good method, stick with it."

## holing pressure putts

☐ be confident of your method
☐ eliminate moving parts
☐ keep putterface square

Holing pressure putts isn't a matter of inherited talent or divine inspiration. It is mostly a question of confidence, and to me confidence is just a word for having a method of doing something that I know will work for you most of the time. Consequently, my first can possibly atone for a missed shot someplace else on tl a missed putt is lost forever.

If there are two basic keys to the Nicklaus approa( be setting up with comfort and confidence and then head and body as still as Augusta, Ga., at midnight. T thing any golfer should do in his putting method.

Nicklaus has been known to use a putter out of a tr; seem amateurish at first glance, but it can be most eff would never do this unless the trap is flat and there hanging lip to the bunker. This can be real good when right for a putter shot and when the cup is not far aw says that he will usually hit the bunker putt more on t| club, making it roll more evenly when coming onto the (

I truly like the Nicklaus method on the green. I can why more amateur golfers don't follow his pattern. It' wouldn't try to copy his style exactly, but his ideas ar more people would check the clutch putts he's made a few tournaments he blew by three-putting, they mi( toward Jack's method.

Yet Jack himself has cautioned against taking to( from others. Not long ago, he said something that r sense to me.

"Advice is the commonest and cheapest com( golf course. One place to completely ignore it is on 1 ways do your own thinking on putts. No one else kn you are going to hit the ball, so there's no way they your line. Besides, a lot of discussion about 'bre; tention from distance, which I believe is the critical f the world as you prepare to putt, then do your own tl can possibly atone for a missed shot someplace else on the hole, but a missed putt is lost forever.

If there are two basic keys to the Nicklaus approach, it would be setting up with comfort and confidence and then keeping his head and body as still as Augusta, Ga., at midnight. That's something any golfer should do in his putting method.

Nicklaus has been known to use a putter out of a trap. This may seem amateurish at first glance, but it can be most effective. Jack would never do this unless the trap is flat and there is no overhanging lip to the bunker. This can be real good when the bunker is right for a putter shot and when the cup is not far away. Nicklaus says that he will usually hit the bunker putt more on the toe of the club, making it roll more evenly when coming onto the grass.

I truly like the Nicklaus method on the green. I can't understand why more amateur golfers don't follow his pattern. It's so sound. I wouldn't try to copy his style exactly, but his ideas are excellent. If more people would check the clutch putts he's made and recall how few tournaments he blew by three-putting, they might lean more toward Jack's method.

Yet Jack himself has cautioned against taking too much advice from others. Not long ago, he said something that makes a lot of sense to me.

"Advice is the commonest and cheapest commodity on the golf course. One place to completely ignore it is on the greens. Always do your own thinking on putts. No one else knows how hard you are going to hit the ball, so there's no way they can determine your line. Besides, a lot of discussion about 'break' diverts attention from distance, which I believe is the critical factor. Shut out the world as you prepare to putt, then do your own thing."

# 8
# george
# archer

Most of his fellow-professionals say that if they had a putt of eight feet or less that absolutely had to be made, the man they would choose to make it is George Archer. His reputation for holing pressure putts spans a career that began in 1964 and includes one Masters title, 11 tour victories and earnings of over $800,000.

Archer's ability with the putting blade is remarkable in view of his gangly, 6-6 frame. Most outstanding putters are built much closer to the ground. George has the ability few tall men can muster of keeping his body still, a technique he discusses in this chapter.

Archer would not advocate that everyone putt like he does. "I'd say give my method a try, and if it works as well for you as it does for me, then we're both happy," Archer states. "If it doesn't work, look around for something else. But once you've found a good method, stick with it."

## holing pressure putts

☐ be confident of your method
☐ eliminate moving parts
☐ keep putterface square

Holing pressure putts isn't a matter of inherited talent or divine inspiration. It is mostly a question of confidence, and to me confidence is just a word for having a method of doing something that you know will work for you most of the time. Consequently, my first rule of putting is to know exactly what I am trying to do. My second rule is to stay faithful to my proven method, even when it isn't working too well.

I'm sure one of the big reasons I've achieved something in golf is because usually I've been able to make myself stick to what I know will work for me. A lot of fellows develop a good game, then when they bring it on tour and see the other players do something different, they try to change. You have to have the strength of will not to mess around with what you've been taught or what you've already proved is right for you.

I know a lot of the tour pros think exactly the opposite to me about the putting stroke. That's fine. They are using what they have discovered works for them. So am I. And so should every golfer.

My putting action is closely related to my action with all the other clubs. Simplicity of method is essential to be able to constantly repeat actions. Thus I see the putting stroke, not as a variation from the basic golf swing, but as a miniature edition of it. The fundamentals of alignment, posture and swing path I apply with a driver, or a 5-iron, I also apply on a smaller scale with the putter.

Because of this approach, my putting action involves what some golfers would regard as a major departure from the method commonly used by many tour pros for keeping the clubface "square" to the intended line of the putt throughout the stroke.

Though my method looks the exact reverse of what many theoreticians presently regard as a "square" movement of the putterhead, I am convinced that it is sound.

Up to the point of actually moving the club away from the ball, I employ many of the accepted putting basics. For example, I use a reverse overlap grip in which my left forefinger lays across my right little finger. This allows the hands to work as a single unit. I place my hands on the club with the back of the left hand and the palm of the right parallel to the putterface, and lay both thumbs straight down the top of the grip (flat-topped on my putter). To avoid the right hand overpowering the left — a sure way to pull putts — I grip the club slightly more firmly in my left hand than my right. Usually I have the feeling that I am controlling the stroke with my left hand. This helps keep the putter low to the ground — like when brushing the floor — and makes for a smoother-rolling putt.

On all putts I address the ball fractionally inside (right of) my left

To stabilize his body and head and eliminate sway during the putting stroke, George Archer flexes his knees and bends from the waist. He describes the posture as "sitting in a chair" because the sensation it produces is similar to lowering yourself into a seat.

toe, my weight favoring my left leg. This weight distribution also reduces any tendency to pull the ball left of target. I regard a "square" set-up as essential in directing the ball accurately and without need for complicated compensations. In putting, as in setting up to most other shots, I draw imaginary lines through my toes, knees, hips and shoulders, and try to place myself so that they are all parallel to the first two or three feet of the shot. Usually I stand with my feet about six inches apart, which allows me to feel comfortable and well balanced. I try to position my head so that the bridge of my nose is directly over the ball, enabling me to look directly down on it. I locate my hands opposite the crease of my left trouser leg, which, related to the position of the ball, ensures that the putter shaft is vertical, and that I will contact the ball at the lowest point of the swing, rather than chopping down or hitting up at it.

I discovered as an amateur that the fewer moving parts I employ, the simpler I can keep my stroke and the better I can concen-

Archer prefers a "stroking" to "popping" action on the greens, especially when the putting surface is fast. His conception of a good rhythm is a pendulum movement.

trate on direction and speed. Therefore, to minimize movement, I lock myself into what I hope is a state of immobility by bending at the knees and waist even more than my height (6'-6") necessitates. I can best describe this position as "sitting in a chair," because it feels very much like lowering yourself into a seat, just before you make contact with it.

There have been fine putters — Arnold Palmer is a good example — who move the club away from and through the ball with a hinging of the wrists, keeping their arms relatively still except on very long putts. This is not for me. I use hardly any wrist action. I swing the club almost entirely with my arms. It's a distinctly pendulum-like movement of the putter, hands and arms all working in unison, or in "one piece," with the shoulders rather than the wrists acting as the pivot or fulcrum. Bob Charles, one of the finest putters in golf, is a perfect example of this type of action, and I've spent a lot of time watching Bob, trying to copy his finely coordinated "one-piece" movement and his smooth, rhythmical motion. The method

69

is essentially a stroking rather than a tapping or "popping" action, and is ideal for the fast, bent-grass greens I grew up on. However, I should warn that I've had trouble on Florida courses where the grainy Bermuda grasses seem to favor players who "pop" the ball sharply, rather than stroking through it pendulum-style.

In all the foregoing areas there is probably nothing about my style of putting that most tour players and teaching professionals wouldn't accept in principle, even if they may personally prefer one or more variations. Where I beg to differ from many of my fellow pros is in what constitutes a "square" alignment of the putterface during the backswing. And it is in this vital dimension, particularly, that I relate the putting action to the full golf swing.

It seems to me that many golfers today attempt to keep the putterface looking in the same direction during the backswing as it faced at address. To maintain this clubface position, they deliberately or unconsciously work the putterhead into what I regard as a "closed" position by using a "turning under" (counter clockwise) movement of the left hand. Golfers who use this technique end up with the putterface tilted or angled towards the ground at the completion of the backswing.

Even though manipulating the putter in this way may work pretty well with practice, I believe golfers who do so are often under a misapprehension as to what they are actually achieving. As I see it they are using a method which, to be effective, requires a compensation. This compensation is a clockwise reversal of the hand and wrist action they used going back, so that they, in effect, "open" the clubface as it returns to the ball. Also, I believe that the "shutting under" action is dangerous because it can so easily cause head and body movement, a chief cause of poor putting.

My concept of a "square" putter swing is best illustrated by the opening and closing action of a door. I believe that when the putterhead is swung back naturally and "squarely" by the hands and arms, with little or no wrist break, the toe of the club will move farther away from the ball than will the heel, just as the handle of a door moves farther away from the jamb than does the hinge side as you swing it open. To make both sides of the door move equally, you would have to shift the hinges also. A golfer's head is his hinge or fulcrum, but it is not immoveable like a hinged door post. I feel he is in serious danger of swaying his head along with the putter when

70

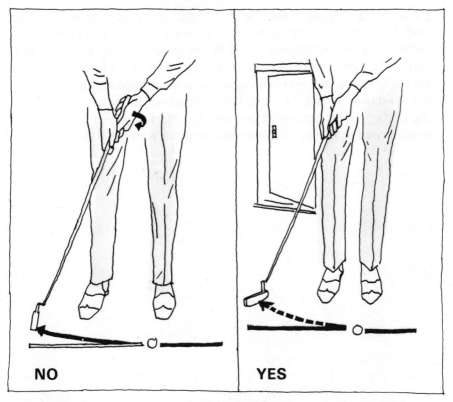

NO  YES

The putterhead, Archer maintains, should not be swung back with counter-clockwise movement of the left hand and wrist in an effort to keep the face "square" to the line of the putt. He says that this action closes the clubface and necessitates a compensating clockwise turn of the hands and wrists in returning the clubface squarely through the ball.

he tries to keep all parts of the clubface the same distance from the ball by "hooding", or turning the clubface under during the backswing.

Do not interpret the above as meaning that I deliberately fan open the clubface on the backswing by rolling my hands and wrists to the right (clockwise) as they swing the putter back. This I seek to avoid at all costs. Such an artifical manipulation of the clubface is even more difficult to control than the "shutting under" action.

In the action I advocate, you neither "open" nor "close" the clubface, but simply swing it back from the ball like an opening door. After it has moved-back about six inches, its toe will have moved about an inch farther than its heel, and the farther you go back, the farther away the toe of the club will move, relative to the heel, from the ball. This is not an "opening" of the clubface, either deliberately or unconsciously. It is the natural result of a correct, one-piece backswing stroke. It allows a return of the clubface squarely to the ball without requiring any compensating turning of the hands and wrists. In short, this method will most naturally return the putter to the position from which it started, which is the basic requirement to make solid, accurate contact with the ball.

# 9

# bruce crampton

Bob Toski of Golf Digest's professional teaching panel labels Bruce Crampton "the most underrated putter in the game." Jack Nicklaus calls Crampton "a super putter."

Crampton, a native Australian who now lives in Dallas, joined the American pro tour in 1957 at the age of 20. He became known as golf's "iron man" because he played in so many events. His parents had wanted him to take up their game, tennis, but Bruce opted for golf. He has had six consecutive years of winning more than $100,000, overcoming a rocky early career, spanning five years, in which he could not make expenses in 80 starts. He has since won 14 tour events.

In this chapter, Crampton explains the approach to putting that has helped him win over a million dollars and tells you how you can apply his successful techniques to your game.

## putt with confidence

- ☐ picture putt in your mind
- ☐ rid yourself of tension
- ☐ stroke short putts solidly

There is no substitute for confidence in putting. In my mental processes before I step up to a putt I'm certainly not looking for ways to miss it.

But you can't think a putt into the hole. A good mental attitude

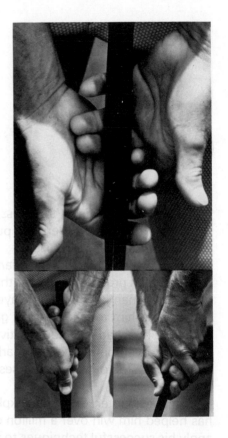

Bruce Crampton's grip is in the fingers, the club handle under the heel pad of his left hand. When he closes his hands, the palms are square to the line and the thumbs straight up and down the shaft. He uses the reverse overlap grip with the left forefinger.

must complement good mechanics. Couple a good technique with good thoughts and you've got something.

When you are preparing to make a crucial putt you should be thinking about how you're going to make it. You don't think, "Gee whiz, that looks like a tough putt." Once a negative thought gets in your mind and you start looking for a way to miss the putt, you often will miss it. When things are going well you never think about missing those putts you should make. All that's in your mind is how you're going to make them.

I'm often a poor putter on bad greens. But in 1973 at both Tucson and Houston, where most players were talking about how hard the greens were to putt, I told myself I was playing the best golf and was a good putter and had the better chance of putting a good solid stroke on the ball, and if I did, it would go in. I won both tournaments.

Here are some positive thoughts that can help you.

Play picture golf. Try to see the line and see the ball going into the hole. Try to keep this picture in your mind. It's a form of self-hypnosis. You're more than halfway to putting it in.

Accept the fact that you have no control over the ball once it leaves the putter. There is no use worrying about bumps or spike marks or anything else that might happen once the ball leaves the putter. Your thoughts should be about putting the putterface on the ball in the best possible manner. That's all you can do about it.

Rid yourself of tension. Tension comes from insecurity, from the fear of missing. You never are completely free from tension under pressure. I know I'm not, even though I've made many putts for money in crucial situations. But if you're concentrating on how to make the putt rather than on what will happen if you miss, you will be more relaxed.

Be decisive. When you're worried at the last second that a spike mark might kick the ball one way or the other, when you're not quite sure what the line is, you can't form that positive picture in your mind. If I get a line in mind and my caddie tells me something different, then I've got that indecision. That's why I line up my own putts. You'll be able to put a much better stroke on the ball and have a much greater chance of holing the putt if you make up your mind and stick to it.

Don't be too careful on short putts. That sounds like strange advice, but those three-to-five footers are the toughest putts in golf because we know we should make them. We get too careful, then we try to guide or wish the ball in, instead of thinking, "All I've got to do is start it on this line with a solid stroke and it's going to go in "

The putter: I prefer a mallet-type putter to a blade, because I think I get a livelier feel. But the choice of a putter is an individual matter. If you feel you can putt well with a broomstick, that's what I'd suggest you use.

The grip: I grip the putter in the fingers of both hands, keeping the handle under the heel pad of the left hand. I use the reverse overlap grip, with both thumbs placed straight up and down the shaft, which puts the palms of my hands more square to the line.

The stance: Be comfortable. My right foot is slightly ahead of my left. I'm more comfortable with this open stance. Whatever type of stance you use you must be well-balanced.

The key to Crampton's stroke with the arms and the shoulders is that the angles of the wrists do not change as everything moves through the stroke as a unit. Note the position of the golf ball just inside the ball of his left foot at address. His thumbs

Your eyes must be over the top of the target line and slightly behind the ball. Be sure you're looking at the back of the ball. That's where the putter is going to make contact. Too many people look at the top of the ball.

Your arms should hang almost straight down, elbows tucked in naturally, your hands just far enough from your body so they clear your thighs during the stroke.

I don't think you'll ever putt well with your hands behind the ball. You can pull something straighter than you can push it. To insure that your hands are leading the club, I suggest that you place the ball just inside the ball of your left foot and check to make sure your thumbs are near the crease in the left leg of your pants, as I do.

The stroke: The key to putting is hitting the ball solidly. I'm an arms-and-shoulders putter and I feel that if you putt this way you'll hit it solidly more consistently than a player who uses a wrist stroke.

I'm not stiff, but I don't think the outside angles formed by the hands and arms should change at all on putts in the 10-to-15 foot range . . . and very little on longer putts. There should be no flippiness, no breakdown of the left wrist.

76

are near the pants crease of his left leg, placing the hands ahead of the clubface. His eyes are slightly behind the ball. The head and body stay still during the swing. The putterhead is low throughout, especially at the finish of this 12-foot putt.

My left hand dominates the stroke, initiating the backswing, guiding and keeping the club extending through the ball toward the target with a constant, slightly accelerating stroke. The major fault with the average player's putting stroke is that he quits with the left hand. Avoid this and you will make more putts. If you can extend your left hand through toward the target, you will make more putts.

This dominant left hand enables you to keep the putter lower during the swing so you hit the ball with a level stroke. If your hands are behind the clubhead or your left wrist breaks down before impact, the club will come up and you'll get a weaker hit. On shorter putts, when I'm putting well, I even find the putter finishing on the ground.

You must start your backswing from motion to be smooth. I use a slight up-and-down tapping motion and an almost imperceptible forward press of the hands to get my putter started.

Keep your body still, especially on those crucial shorter putts.

Take the putter back and through as straight as you can along the target line. Constantly remind yourself to keep your backstroke short to avoid easing up on the putt coming through the ball.

On longer putts, where touch and speed are important, keep your grip rather light. But on the shorter putts, where it is crucial to be accurate and the stroke is more compact, it is important to maintain uniform pressure. If you grip the club lightly at address you've got to tense a little to take it away. This will change the angle of the club. So grip the club a little firmer on the short ones . . . not rigid, but firm. Then you can draw it back without changing that grip pressure.

I also sometimes grip down on the shaft on shorter putts for better control.

Once you have a correct mechanical approach, it is up to you to practice sufficiently so that when you stand over a putt your muscle memory will take over and you'll make the stroke without thinking about it. If you asked a baseball pitcher to think about the position of his elbow while he's throwing, he'd never get the ball over the plate. The same holds true in putting.

The speed's the thing — I'm a speed putter. Once you've decided the break and formed a mental picture of the ball rolling into the hole, just think about rolling the ball at the correct speed.

How do you determine the correct speed? My thought is that you strike the ball just hard enough so it will hit the back of the cup lightly. This will allow you to use all the hole; if the ball is slightly off-line it still can topple in. If you try to knock the ball boldly at the back of the cup and you're slightly off-center it's going to lip out.

Applying the proper speed is a matter of feel and touch, and I've noticed that a person doing hard work or lifting heavy weights usually won't have the sensitivity to get the ball rolling as well as a dentist or physician or somebody doing delicate work with his hands. I know I'll probably putt better on Sunday than I will on Tuesday, because I unload my car early in the week. Avoid heavy work the next time you have an important match coming up.

# part II
# proven principles of the great putters

# 10
# proven putting principles

In the preceding chapters, you have read the personal techniques of a gallery of golf's greatest putters. Their techniques may differ in some respects, but most agree that certain fundamentals are essential to sound putting. In this chapter, the editors gather these fundamentals under three headings—grip, stance and stroke, explaining the common elements that govern the putting styles of all the master putters.

## grip

☐ place thumbs down the shaft
☐ grip lightly for 'feel'
☐ keep back of left hand facing hole

If you were to spend a day or so around the practice putting green during one of the major golf tournaments—for instance, the Masters or the U.S. Open—you would see what at first might appear to you as a bewildering variety of ways to grip a putter. This would be true even if you confined your observations to those players with conventional putting styles, and did not take into account the rare ones who putt cross-handed, or side-saddle fashion, or with the hands separated on the club by several inches.

Most of the experts agree that the soundest putting grip has the palms facing each other with the right palm and back of the left hand facing down the putting line.

On closer examination, you would see that the putting grips of virtually all the leading players have one main thing in common. And if you had the opportunity to hear each one describe the basics of his putting grip, you would note a remarkable similarity of opinion on this common point:

"In developing a proper grip you should strive to position your hands so that the palms oppose, or face, each other on the putter shaft. . . . With the palms opposed . . . the putterblade can be kept square to the line much more easily." (Bill Casper)

"The back of the left hand faces the line of the putt." (Bob Rosburg)

Arnold Palmer favors having the back of his left hand facing the hole, with palms facing each other. Deane Beman recommends keeping the hands in similar juxtaposition. George Archer strives to strike the ball with the blade square by keeping the back of his left hand and the palm of his right facing the hole. Bob Charles, another expert, also favors palms in opposition.

And so on down the line, with an occasional exception that amounts more to a personal modification than a different concept. For instance, Jerry Barber keeps the back of his left hand facing the hole, while his right hand is turned just a bit more under the shaft than is the case with those mentioned above. The back of Jack Nicklaus' left hand looks slightly left of target to help him avoid pulling putts.

82

The most commonly used grip is the reverse overlap (left) in which the forefinger of the left hand overlaps the little finger or last two fingers of the right hand. Many players, such as Bob Rosburg and Art Wall, favor the "ten-finger" grip in which every finger is on the shaft (right) because they believe this grip gives them better control.

Great golfers of the past confirm this principle. The late Horton Smith came out four-square for having the back of the left hand facing the intended line directly, with the palms exactly opposing. Paul Runyan believed the hands should oppose each other, although, like Barber, he added a modification of his own. Runyan set the left hand and the right hand farther under the shaft than would be considered standard, but held to the theory of the hands opposing each other.

Out of the more distant past, and from England, Joyce Wethered, whom many regard as the greatest woman player in the history of golf, theorized similarly: "Keep the back of the left hand facing toward the hole rather than showing on top of the shaft and the back of the right hand at the same time well behind the shaft."

The same reasoning underlies the precepts laid down by Robert T. "Bobby" Jones Jr., who, in addition to being one of the greatest golfers of all time, was also one of the most articulate.

Jones emphasized a grip with the thumbs on top of the shaft, the back of the left hand and the palm of the right facing the hole. This positioning is intended to avoid twisting the clubface out of alignment with the line of the putt.

Like Jones, virtually all distinguished authorities on putting stress placing the thumbs straight down the top of the shaft. With the back of the left hand and the palm of the right hand facing directly along the intended line, the natural position for the thumbs will be straight down the top of the shaft.

A number of great putters stress the role that the thumbs—the right thumb, in particular—play in the putting stroke. Bobby Jones theorized that pressing only the tip-end joint of the right thumb, not its whole length, to the club provided a sensitive touch that results in accurate putting control. A few experts like Johnny Farrell went even further, exerting pressure on the club only with the end of the thumb. Farrell also pressed his thumbnail into the grip.

This stress on thumb placement assumes greater significance when considering the George Low technique. Several years ago he virtually abandoned all phases of golf except putting, at which he is an acknowledged wizard. He claims he can beat anybody in the world in putting, and is rarely challenged to prove it.

Low says that the key to his uncanny ability to putt is in the thumbs. Low places only the first joint of both the right and left thumbs on top of the shaft and presses downward with them, with a light but clearly defined pressure.

Both Casper and Nicklaus, two of the finest putters of the last decade, say they "feel" the putt through the right thumb and forefinger, which is poised almost as if it were a trigger finger on the putting shaft.

All of this lends credence to the theory that thumb place - ment and pressure have a lot to do with developing an effective putting grip. The golfer who aspires to be an outstanding putter, or even just a better putter than he is, would do well to check his own grip with a view to making the adjustments suggested above.

There are endless variations of "proper" putting grips. The most widely used method of placing the hands on the club is called the "reverse overlap" grip. In it the index finger of the left hand overlaps the little finger of the right hand, whereas in the regular overlap grip, the little finger of the right hand overlaps the index finger of the left hand.

Billy Casper, a leading exponent of the reverse overlap method, grips the club with the index finger of the left hand overlapping both the little finger and the third finger of the right hand. He says the basic aim of the putting grip is to develop a sensitive feel with the right hand, which he considers the dominant hand in the putting

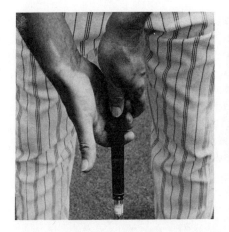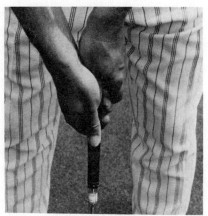

Almost without exception, all great putters agree that a good putting grip has the thumbs of both hands going straight down the top of the shaft. This promotes better touch and square alignment.

stroke, while the left hand's main function is to steady the stroke and keep the face of the putter square to the line.

Bruce Crampton, Jack Nicklaus, Bob Charles and George Archer all employ the reverse overlap grip. Gary Player and Arnold Palmer use a variation in which the index finger of the left hand is extended straight down to its full length. Many other good putters employ this variation, in the belief that the fully extended left index finger makes a good lever for initiating the backswing.

Bobby Locke uses the regular overlapping grip, usually referred to as the Vardon grip, identical to the one he and most other top flight golfers employ for full shots.

Bob Rosburg and Art Wall Jr., two of the very best on the greens, use the ten-finger grip for putting as well as for all their other shots. "I follow the principle of gripping the putter just as I do the rest of my clubs," says Rosburg, "on the theory that this feels most normal." Other experts agree that there is probably an advantage in using the same basic grip for putting as for the other shots, since the putting stroke is essentially a shortened version of the full swing.

Another grip used by a considerable number of golfers but rarely seen among the pros calls for overlapping the little and third fingers of the right hand over the index and middle fingers of the left hand. This grip leaves the left hand in a stronger position than the right, which contradicts the putting theories of most experts.

Several years ago Gene Sarazen began using a grip whose distinguishing feature was that the right index finger was fully extended and positioned along the right side of the shaft. Sarazen called it the "after-40 finger grip." He recommended its use particularly to older golfers as a better means of steadying the stroke. Many golfers use this grip, although Sarazen himself has not stuck with it consistently.

Perhaps it should be noted here that a number of name golfers over the years have recommended a particular putting grip with which they were having success at the time, then changed to another grip or reverted to an old method shortly afterward. In fact, most golfers continually experiment with various putting methods and gimmicks, discovering that what may work well for a while does not necessarily stand the test of time.

The most curious putting grips presently being used with conspicuous success are those of Phil Rodgers and Englishman Paul Trevillion.

Rodgers uses what he calls the "split-grip" technique. He holds the very end of the putter with his left hand tight against his belt, keeping this hand stationary throughout the stroke. His right hand is about a foot below the left, and his grip with the right hand is with the thumb and first three fingers, using a very delicate pressure. The basic purpose of this grip is. to achieve a pendulum motion with the putter.

Trevillion carries this method to extremes, using a sawed-off putter and splitting his hands much the same as Rodgers and Runyan, but closer to the ground. Rodgers learned the split grip from Runyan, who still recommends it highly. At first, Runyan found it very effective on putts of up to 15 feet, but less so on longer putts. Then he began using a putter with a shaft about 41 inches long, some 6 inches longer than the regular puttershaft length. This longer putter — Rodgers' putter is of similar length — enabled Runyan to produce a controlled stroke even on long putts requiring a more forceful stroke.

The cross-handed putting grip, also called the reverse-handed grip, began to enjoy a considerable vogue about 1965. Fred Haas Jr., the veteran New Orleans professional who became the United States Seniors champion in 1965, had been using the technique for several years. It was subsequently adopted by such successful pros

The cross-handed putting grip has been used successfully by players like Orville Moody ( right ) and Mary Mills because they feel this makes it easier for the left wrist to remain in control during the putting stroke. In the cross-handed grip, the left hand is positioned below the right.

as Johnny Pott, Orville Moody, Wes Ellis Jr., Peter Alliss of Great Britain's Ryder Cup team, and, among the ladies, Marilynn Smith and Mary Mills, the 1973 LPGA Champion.

As its name implies, the essential feature of this grip is that the hands are crossed, or reversed from their normal position. The right hand is placed on top and the left hand below it by right-handed golfers. There are minor variations of this grip. Ellis describes his own:

"My grip is the interlocking, with the little finger of my left hand twining around the forefinger of my right hand. This is simply a left-handed interlock as might be used by any left-hander. I putt right-handed, however. The back of my left hand and the palm of my right hand face toward the hole. My thumbs are directly on top of the shaft. Both hands feel the same amount of tension. My hands seem to fit more closely together with the interlock, but I don't think it makes any difference as to the particular kind of grip used so long as it is basically cross-handed. A player simply should experiment until he finds the grip that feels most comfortable for him.

"The thing that has improved my putting since I adopted the cross-handed method is the fact that now my left hand and wrist remain firm and in control. The right hand never 'takes over,' causing the left wrist to collapse at impact. The face of the putter remains square to the line for a longer time without any special effort on my part to keep it square. Thus I now feel I have a better chance of putting the ball along the line I selected."

Johnny Pott uses several individual variations which seem to help his personal putting efficiency. First, he places only two of the fingers of his left hand on the club itself, overlapping the other two over his lower two right fingers. Then he uses a flat-top putter grip, with both thumbs placed on it. He also guards against too strong influence by his right hand, keeping his left hand in control in order to prevent closing the face of the club or pushing the ball on impact.

Both Moody and Pott scored notable successes on the pro tour, and their comments make it clear that the cross-handed grip can be used effectively. They also indicate that the golfer who chooses to experiment with this grip should work out his own variations of its minor details. The same would doubtless be true of both the Runyan-Rodgers split grip and the so-called conventional grip.

After the golfer works out his own best method of placing his hands on the club, he must still determine how tightly to grip it. In the opinion of most experts, most average golfers grip the club too tightly, so tightly, in fact, that they set up muscular tension in the forearms, ruining their chances of achieving a fluid, smooth putting stroke.

The general advice usually supplied is that the club should be held firmly enough to assure complete control at all times, yet not so firmly as to set up undue tension. Many golfers, beginners in particular, would probably find this advice too vague and need something more specific. Trying to be more graphic, some experts have said that the amount you would use in holding a small bird in order not to let it get away and yet not to hurt it.

Another problem to be considered is whether gripping pressure should be evenly distributed. Should more pressure be applied with one hand than the other, or should extra pressure be applied with certain fingers? Logic would require your holding the club a bit more firmly with the left hand than the right, since the left hand is used mainly to steady the club and keep it correctly aligned, while the right hand basically propels the clubhead and regulates the force with which the ball is hit. Since you depend chiefly on the right hand for touch, the grip pressure with this hand should be quite delicate. Most experts do agree that the pressure executed by the left hand, particularly the last three fingers, should slightly exceed that exerted by the right.

Bobby Jones, for example, has emphasized the danger of tenseness in a putting grip, maintaining that the left hand alone should firmly grip the club. Jones used only the last three fingers of the left hand to achieve this firmness.

One point easily overlooked is that the gripping muscles will naturally tighten as the clubhead is taken away from the ball and the clubhead's weight begins to be sensed by the controlling muscles. Taking this into account, you should make the grip at address quite light, since it will naturally tighten somewhat as the actual stroke begins.

Dave Stockton, one of the tour's finest putters, also advocates a light grip, particularly with the right hand. "The right hand grip should be entirely with the fingers," he says.

Bob Toski, a former World Champion and now one of golf's preeminent teachers, believes most golfers grip too tightly.

"People can't believe how lightly they can and should grip the putter and still maintain control," Toski says. "The putting stroke, like all others, is a swinging motion. How tight do you have to grip the putter in order to lift it off the ground? Most poor players try to over-control the putter with their hands instead of holding the putter very lightly and swinging the club back and forth. Surely putting is the most delicate of strokes and the one requiring the greatest sensitivity in the hands and fingers. A strong, tight grip merely destroys the sensitivity and feel necessary for good putting."

The golfer who suspects that his putting troubles may stem from his gripping the putter too tightly or too loosely (this latter fault is much more rare) should go to the practice green and try out various grip pressures to determine the one that best suits him.

Common variations of stance used by golfers include (left to right) the open stance, in which the front foot is pulled several inches farther away from the target line than the back foot; the square stance, in which the toes of both feet are lined up parallel to the intended line; and the closed stance, in which the back foot is drawn several inches farther than the front from the putting line.

# stance

☐ get proper perspective on line
☐ achieve comfort and balance
☐ look directly down at ball

An effective putting stance has three basic, interrelated components:

First, you must stand so that the ball and the hole are in proper perspective. That is, you must be able to look from the ball directly along the line it must travel to reach the hole.

Second, the stance must assure you balance and stability. This ties in with perspective, since if you move (reposition) the body during the stroke, you will not have the same perspective you started with, and consequently will have a different alignment with your target.

Third, you must be as comfortable as possible, while still maintaining proper perspective, balance and stability. Comfort in this case, of course, means the absense of any strain or cramp—the sort

90

that allows maximum freedom of movement to the arms and hands while keeping the rest of the body stationary.

Any given putting stance may emphasize one of these components over the other two. For instance, the open stance, in which the right foot is advanced from one to several inches closer to the target line than the left, affords a slightly better perspective because the body more nearly faces the hole. This makes it easier to sight along the intended line by moving the head back and forth.

In regard to perspective, then, the open is superior to the closed stance. With a closed stance, the right foot is pulled back one to several inches behind the left, which naturally turns the body slightly away from the target. But the closed stance, because it also moves the right hip back, affords more freedom of movement for the arms on the backswing.

The square stance, in which the toes of both feet are on a line parallel with the intended line of the putt, is a compromise between the open and closed stances, embodying, but not emphasizing, the best and worst features of each.

The golfer encounters another problem in deciding on how far apart to place his feet. Spreading the feet wide apart naturally provides better balance and stability. But by doing so he also tends to stretch and tense the muscles of his back and shoulders, thereby taking something away from his sense of touch, or feel.

All of this is prefatory to saying that putting stances vary greatly, even among the very best putters, and is intended to explain to some extent why they do. Billy Casper and Bobby Locke, two of the greatest putters that golf has ever known, favor a slightly closed stance. It is probable that both have extraordinary peripheral vision with no problem in scanning the line of their putts and, therefore, prefer to emphasize freedom of movement on the backswing.

Bob Rosburg uses a slightly open stance, but he couples it with a short putting backswing and consequently has no need to be concerned about the right hip getting in the way when he takes the club back.

Johnny Revolta, a super-putter in his prime, adopted a very open putting stance, so open that on especially long putts where he needed to take a long backswing he risked hitting his right foot with the head of his putter. It may be significant that, using this putting stance, he was excellent on short- or medium-range putts but had some trouble on the long approach putts.

The width of the stance varies enormously among successful putters, from the "spread-eagle" stance of Hubert Green and Ruth Jessen, who place their feet more than a yard apart, to several who place their feet so close together that they almost touch. Bobby Jones, who stressed comfort above all else, favored a very narrow stance, maintaining that he found it the most comfortable. Lloyd Mangrum, a great putter in his prime, stood with his feet not more than half an inch apart. Arnold Palmer's stance is also quite narrow. Billy Casper places his feet about 12 inches apart, which could be designated the medium range. So do Crampton, Jerry Barber and most of the other players on the professional tour.

As noted earlier, a prime consideration in taking the stance is achieving balance and stability. This is what Palmer is seeking by turning both knees inward to brace himself against any possible body movement. The tendency to move the body on the backswing is slight. It is far less a threat than the tendency to move the body laterally in the direction of the hole as the clubhead is started forward to strike the ball, which is a particular danger in tense situa-

The width of the stance varies greatly among golf's top putters. Some favor a very wide stance, like young Brian Allin (right) whose feet are more than 30 inches apart. Others like Lloyd Mangrum (left) prefer a narrow stance in which the feet are only an inch or two apart.

tions. Anxiety makes it difficult to stand rock steady until the ball is hit and on its way.

Players try to guard against sway in different ways. Jack Nicklaus' solution is to stand with the bulk of his weight on the right foot. To a lesser degree, so did Cary Middlecoff. England's Joyce Wethered also advocated a putting stance in which most of the weight was on the right side.

"The question of stance must be decided," Miss Wethered said, "with a view, first, to finding the best position in which the balance of the body can be controlled. On the whole, it is preferable to keep the weight on the back of the right foot, and well back on the heels, in order to prevent the dangerous practice of swaying forward during the stroke. It is easier in this way to maintain the necessary tension of the body until the stroke is completed. The important thing to note is that the hold of the feet on the ground determines the steadiness of the body—a vitally necessary form of support when such a very delicate action as putting is being carried

Virtually all the putting experts agree that you should have the eyes directly over the ball and the line of the putt, as does Jerry Barber in this photo. If your putting is poor, this is one of the first places to look for correction.

out with the hands. No swaying of the upper part of the body must be allowed during the stroke; even after the ball is hit, it is dangerous."

But despite Nicklaus' example and Joyce Wethered's eloquence on the subject, a majority of good putters prefer to stand with more weight on the left side than the right. Casper advocates distributing weight either evenly on both feet, or slightly favoring the left side. Jerry Barber and George Low put most of their weight on the left side.

Arnold Palmer is one of the many who stand with the weight equally distributed on both feet, but he emphasizes having the weight to the inside (near the instep) rather than to the outside.

Paradoxical as it may seem, golfers who stand with most of their weight on the left side are also trying to guard against swaying the body laterally in the direction of the hole. They simply view the problem differently from those who favor the right side, reasoning that if the bulk of the weight is on the left side to begin with, there will be less tendency to shift to that direction during the stroke.

The point is that there are excellent putters who elect to stand with the weight on the right side, on the left side, or equally distributed. It is, like so many other things in putting, something that each player must work out for himself.

The same rule applies to width of stance. In this connection, some authorities favor a fairly wide stance for long putts and a narrow one for short putts. In fact, nearly all good putters—Billy Casper is a case in point—widen their basic stance to some degree when the putt is a very long one and a long backswing is required.

Regarding stance and posture, there is one point that virtually all good putters have in common: they stand so that their eyes are directly above the ball. "This makes for better coordination between hands and eyes," says Cary Middlecoff. "If you are bending too far forward so that the eyes will look straight down at a point beyond the ball, your chances of putting consistently well are slim indeed. The same is true if your stance is so upright that you will look straight down at a point between your feet and the ball." Middlecoff adds, "If you find your putting game gone suddenly bad, this is probably the most likely place to look for correction."

Jack Nicklaus agrees. "Looking directly down at the ball is vital for me. If my eyes are out beyond the ball, I tend to pull putts left. If my eyes are inside the line, I tend to push putts right."

Having the eyes directly over the ball is, of course, quite logical. When scanning the path you want the ball to travel, you obviously want your starting point to be where the ball is now. Getting a proper putting perspective and subsequent stroke is more difficult if your eyes are focused anywhere else.

Many good putters prefer to stand to the ball in a way that allows the upper part of their arms to rest, and thus be steadied against the body. A vital feature of an effective putting stance is slightly flexed knees. To lock either knee joint, or worse, both of them, would tense the leg muscles, setting up what would certainly be a stiff and uncomfortable stance.

Bobby Jones favored keeping the arms close to the body with a slight bend in both knees. But at least two great putters partially disagreed with the principle of drawing the arms in close to the body and resting them against the sides. Jerry Barber sets his left arm out from his body, with his left elbow pointing in the direction of the hole. And a putting genius of an earlier era defied the principle altogether. The late Leo Diegel, whose best years were the early

1920's, kept both arms out from the body, with the left elbow pointing toward the hole and the right one pointing in the opposite direction. Diegel's was perhaps the most bizarre putting stance in golf history until the "croquet" and "side-saddle" methods began to gain adherents in recent years.

Writing about putting nearly a half century ago, Joyce Wethered observed: "The player has many difficulties to contend with. He is neither on the same level as the ball, nor behind it, but above and at a particularly awkward angle for getting a clear view of the line. These details add very considerably to the difficulty of aiming or striking correctly."

Such concern may well have led to the development of the side-saddle method. As Miss Wethered suggested, the player cannot get on the same level with the ball (the rules prohibit billiard-like putting). Using the side-saddle method, the player stands facing the hole, no longer positioning himself "at a peculiarly awkward angle for getting a clear view of the line."

Putting stances obviously vary greatly. The fact that a particular stance works for one golfer is no assurance that it will work for another. Probably the best advice is to stick with your present stance if it works for you; if not, try a number of other stances until you find one that suits you.

# stroke

☐ swing with smooth tempo

☐ keep blade square

☐ strike ball solidly

We come now to the actual striking of the ball with the putter. In considering this phase of the putting process, the player should give thought to three main points:

First, the overall stroke should be smooth, rhythmic, fluid. It should be in no way hurried, jerky, frantic. It should have tempo.

Second, the face of the putter should be square (at right angles) to the intended line of roll when it contacts the ball.

Third, the ball should be struck solidly; contact should be made between the center of gravity of the clubface and the back of the ball.

96

Setting up a proper tempo is the first thing to be accomplished as you start the stroking process. Having set yourself comfortably over the ball, make a few preliminary movements as you scan the line along which you intend to roll the ball. These movements correspond to the waggle, which is the name given the back and forth movements you make preliminary to hitting a longer shot.

Many golfers first set the putterhead behind the ball, then in front of the ball, then behind it again, and from that last movement go into the backswing. Others, waggle the clubhead—either back and forth or up and down, or sometimes both—while keeping the head of the putter always behind the ball. It doesn't matter which of these waggling techniques you use.

What is important is to precede the actual backswing with a certain amount of movement. To stand immobilized over the ball and then go abruptly into the backswing robs you of rhythmic tempo. You will jab or stab your putts instead of stroking them. Casper observes on this point:

"To insure that my stroke is free of tension and is as rhythmic as possible, I employ a little up-and-down waggle with the putter blade behind the ball. This little maneuver often goes unnoticed, but it has a very definite purpose: that of helping me take the putter blade back as smoothly as possible, and to ensure a proper line to the hole. This movement is actually the beginning of my putting stroke. . . . Other golfers employ similar movements which are largely designed for the same purpose."

As you make these preliminary movements, being careful to keep them smooth and unhurried, think of them as leading you into a smooth, unhurried start of the backstroke. Bear in mind that there is a natural tendency to speed up the putting stroke as it goes along, particularly if it is a crucial one, so you certainly don't want to rush your stroke at the start.

All good putters stress the need for a smooth, rhythmic tempo. There is much difference of opinion, however, about whether the tempo should be slow or brisk. Many putters say that the stroke ought to be a "sweep." Other equally skillful putters prefer a brisk "tap," or, as Bob Rosburg describes it, a "pop."

Those who advocate the long sweeping stroke usually cite Bobby Jones as their spokesman. Jones advocated a long stroke, with a sweeping and flowing motion, as contrasted with a sharp stroke hitting down on the ball. He based this theory on the assumption that a long sweeping motion prevents cutting across the ball or picking up the right hand (which causes cutting). Jones also favored a flat arc for the putterblade.

Some players feel that the Jones method is out-moded. Paul Runyan observes, "Generally speaking, the more sweeping, pendulum stroke of former days (best exemplified by Bobby Jones) . . . has been replaced by a firmer, more compact hit. By and large, the touch putters of my day have disappeared. They were accomplished enough on long approach putts, but from five and six feet today's tappers are much more accurate. Watch Casper, Rosburg or Sanders and you will see them hit, rather than sweep, the ball."

But the sweep stroke is still favored by many modern players, including Bob Charles and Jerry Barber, two of the finest putters of any era. "I feel strongly," says Barber, "that the stroke should be uninhibited in length. Some players prefer the quick jab or 'pop' style on short putts. Therefore these players must, in effect, develop two putting techniques. I prefer a smooth, unlimited stroke because it works for me on both short and long putts."

Doug Ford, another of the great putters, uses a short, brisk tap regardless of the length of the putt, although naturally he uses a longer backswing for long putts than for short ones. Bob Rosburg makes no distinction between long and short putts, saying simply, "The stroke is a 'pop.'" But he does concede that the long sweeping stroke can be used with great effectiveness. He notes that Bobby Locke, whom he described as "the best putter in the world when he played the tour in the late 1940's," advocates a flowing pendulum stroke using the arms.

These contrasting views reveal that, regarding tempo, there are two sharply distinct schools of thought. Those who favor a brisk tempo are generally found among wrist putters (Casper, Rosburg, Palmer, et al.). Those who use a longer stroke, and therefore a slower tempo, tend to be arm-and-shoulder putters (Charles, Locke, Archer, et al.).

Casper, who uses elements of both methods, describes them as follows:

"The wrist method involves primarily the movement of the arms and wrists. The arms move very little except on long putts, but the hands are quite active because of the hinging action of the wrists.

"In the arm-and-shoulder style of putting the wrists are frozen, so to speak, and the basic movement comes from the arms and shoulders. The hands are regarded as being part of the shaft and the wrists are locked firmly in place from start to finish, except for extremely long putts, when the wrists are permitted to break slightly."

But a word of warning probably should be injected here lest the reader feel he must make an absolutely clear distinction and elect one style or another, exclusively. "Of course, these are matters of shading," says Runyan. "A tap can be overshortened or hurried into a jab. And if you take the wrists out of the stroke too grimly you can stiffen up too much. Any good point can be overdone."

If you overdo the wrist method, you may frequently find yourself snatching the clubhead back too hurriedly on the backswing. Then what you had intended as a putting stroke will become a frantic jab or stab. If you overdo the arm-and-shoulder technique, you may find yourself drawing the club back so far on the backswing that you have to decrease your tempo as you bring the clubhead back into the ball. In either case, you fail to achieve the desired rhythm, smoothness and fluidity.

Whether you use the wrist method or the arm-and-shoulder method, you still need to be certain that the clubhead is accelerating as it comes into the ball, not slowing down.

"If the backswing becomes too long, the stroke must necessarily be softened coming through in order to stop the ball from going too far," says Runyan. "Such deceleration takes away the tap which gives a putt firmness."

Bob Charles is even more emphatic on this point. "Try always to hit the ball with the clubhead accelerating at impact," he advises. "It is very difficult to hit the ball solidly if the clubhead is losing speed as it approaches the ball. This usually happens when you change your mind midway through the swing. If that occurs, the clubhead tends to waver in mid-stroke and all chances of a solid hit are gone. The last thing I think of before the swing is acceleration of the clubhead before impact."

Jack Nicklaus believes that most very short putts are missed because the golfer quits—eases up on the stroke before or at impact. Here's one tip that Jack says has helped him beat this dread disease. "After determining the line, I aim for a spot just short of the hole over which the ball must travel. Then I consciously stroke the putt firmly, continuing to move the putterhead well through the ball toward my selected spot."

The essence of good putting stroke tempo (timing) is, then, to have the clubhead gradually gaining speed as it comes into the ball, which is also the essence of good timing on swings for all other shots.

Our second basic stroke principle requires that the face of the putter be square with the intended line of roll when the ball is struck. If the face is open (turned outward) when the ball is hit, the putt will go to the right of the intended line. A closed face at impact will send the ball to the left. The square-face principle can be departed from successfully only if the player deliberately aligns himself to the right or left of his target with the intent to compensate by pushing or pulling the putt. Rarely can a player who does this become a successful putter.

The square face at impact is what is contemplated in gripping the club with the back of the left hand facing the line and the back of the right hand opposing it. The intention is to have the hand (and thus the face of the putter) in the same position at impact as at the start of the stroke, and the simplest way to bring this about, is to oppose the hands directly to begin with.

The stance, too, is designed to help attain this same end. We have found that comfort, balance and stability should be its essential features. If the stance position is awkward or strained, or if there is body movement during the stroke, the difficulty of bringing the clubhead squarely into the ball is increased.

This principle leads, naturally and logically, to the backswing.

"The putting stroke should be as simple as possible," says Casper. "The simpler the stroke, the more effective and consistent it will be under pressure." On this point, there is no argument at all among experts, whether they be wrist putters or arm-and-shoulder putters.

The wrist putters strive for simplicity by making the shortest possible stroke that will still generate the power (clubhead speed) necessary to knock the ball to the hole. They reason that the shorter the stroke, the less is apt to go wrong with it.

The arm-and-shoulder putters seek simplicity by keeping wrist

100

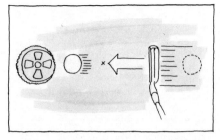

Try always to hit the ball with the putterhead accelerating at impact, to insure a solid hit. Feel your putting stroke go through the ball to a point well beyond it. This is particularly helpful on short putts, which most people ease up on.

break to a minimum. It is obvious that to whatever extent the wrists are cocked on the backswing, they must uncock by that same amount on the forward swing, if the face of the putter is to be square with the line at impact. So if the wrists are largely kept out of the stroke, a longer backswing is required.

It might appear that the ideal putting backswing would carry the clubhead back from the ball in an absolutely straight line. This would be true, however, only if the stroke were started with the hands directly over the ball, with the shaft of the putter perfectly perpendicular to the ground. Then a true pendulum stroke could be achieved, but it would be an awkward and unnatural stroke.

In the normal address position, the hands are held close to the body, setting up an angle of inclination between the hands and the ball. The idea is to maintain the same angle of inclination (plane) on the backswing. In doing this, the clubhead naturally moves a bit inside the line, and the clubface will appear to be slightly open when you reach the end of the backswing. But if you have stayed on the correct plane, the clubface will still be square to the ball. George Archer and George Low liken this action to the hinging of a door or gate.

In the correct and simple putting stroke, the path of the club-head on the forward swing simply retraces the path it took on the backswing. This is natural, uncomplicated and requires no adjust-ments to bring the clubhead into the ball with the face square to the line. You simply go through the ball with the back of the left hand facing the line, as it was when you started the stroke. As a margin of safety, you should keep the back of the left hand facing down the line for a few more inches after the ball is hit.

Bobby Jones considered the follow-through of the left wrist and arm the first requirement of a good putting motion. Bruce Crampton, a "pendulum" putter, and Billy Casper, a "wrist" putter,

One of the key factors in consistent putting is to be sure to line up the face of your putter square to the intended line. This will give you the best chance of returning the putterface squarely to the ball when you hit it.

emphatically agree on this point, despite their different styles: "The right hand should never pass the left until well after the ball has been struck."

While experts generally agree that in a sound putting stroke the left hand dominates the action on the backswing and the right hand on the forward swing, at the same time, they warn against too much conscious emphasis on this point. They counsel against saying to yourself, "I'm going to take the club back with my left hand and hit the ball with my right," because that sort of thinking prohibits your making a smooth, continuous putting stroke in which both hands play their proper roles naturally and spontaneously.

Similar reasoning underlies opinion on taking the putter back low to the ground. Both the sweep putters and the tap putters advocate low backstroking as opposed to picking the clubhead up abruptly, but emphasize once again that a low backstroke is something that should come naturally in the development of a sound putting stroke.

If the face of the putter is closed — looking to the left of the hole (photo at left) — when the ball is hit, the putt will go to the left of the intended line. When the putterface is open — looking to the right of the hole (photo at right) — the ball will go to the right.

A number of the experts have mentioned that when they find themselves putting with loose, flippy wrists, a common putting fault, they concentrate on finishing the stroke with the putter on the ground. This helps firm the left hand through the ball and along the target line. Bobby Jones, Bruce Crampton, Tommy Aaron and Billy Casper have all found this tip useful.

The third basic stroking principle is that the ball must be hit solidly.

"According to my lengthy and close observations," says Cary Middlecoff, "one point held in common by all good putters is that they hit the ball solidly. They almost always bring the center of the clubface into contact with the center of the ball. This has to be an ironclad rule of good putting, because hitting the ball solidly is the only way that 'touch'—the unconscious ability to hit the ball at the desired speed, or momentum—can be achieved. The putter who tends to hit the ball off center must on some occasions hit it more

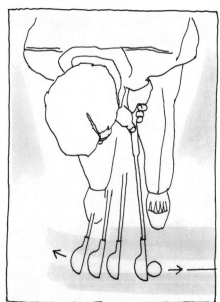

The putterhead should follow the same path on the forward swing that it took on the backswing. This is the most natural and least complicated way to bring the putterface into the ball looking squarely down the intended line.

off center than on others, and only now and then will he hit it in the center. Thus he can never be sure of the amount of force he is getting behind the ball, power being a combination of clubhead speed, clubhead weight, and meeting the ball squarely.''

"Perfect cleanness of striking should be sought before any other consideration," Joyce Wethered maintained. "The ball perfectly hit so that it rolls without any sideway spin will, with remarkable regularity, disappear from view.''

Chief among the several things that contribute to consistently solid hitting of putts is riveting the eyes on the back of the ball and keeping them there until the ball is hit and on its way. Coordination between putterface and ball is paramount.

Second, there must be no body movement during the stroke, as was noted in the section on stance. If the body moves, the head inevitably moves with it, and the eyes cannot remain focused on the ball. Also when the body shifts, the position of the hands with reference to the ball will alter, which will make solid contact considerably more difficult to attain.

Middlecoff pinpoints this as one of the principle reasons poor putters fail to strike the ball solidly.

"Most inexperienced and inconsistent putters move the body

104

Another secret to consistent stroking mentioned by many of the great putters is to keep the left hand and wrist moving through the stroke after impact. Notice in this photo of Bob Murphy how well he extends through the stroke and along the putting line. His left wrist has not collapsed.

forward toward the hole as they strike the putt. This swaying forward shifts the weight to the left foot, causing a blocking action of the hips and wrists. The result is that the player is forced to cut across the ball and push most of his putts to the right," observes Middlecoff.

Third, you must be consistent in your positioning of the ball with reference to the feet. If you play the ball off the left toe at one time, opposite the left instep at another, and occasionally back near the right foot, you cannot set up a consistent stroking pattern.

Virtually all experts agree that the ball should be positioned on a line with the left instep. The ball then lies at the point where, in the natural course of the forward swing, the head of the putter is traveling parallel with the ground.

There have been some successful putters, notably Lloyd Mangrum, who tended to hit down on the ball, and there have been some very good ones who have hit the ball with a slight upward motion as a means of producing extra overspin. But these tactics are certainly exceptions to the general rule; you might even call them idiosyncrasies. The average golfer would undoubtedly be wiser to build his technique around a solid hit in which the head of the putter moves along level with the top of the grass.

A point that is emphasized by almost all the experts is that the putting stroke ought to be basically the same for every putt—a repeating stroke. Only the amount of power applied should vary.

Middlecoff believes it is better to have an essentially unsound putting stroke that you can repeat each time than to be inconsistent with a basically sound stroke. He cites the case of Dave Douglas: "Dave cut all his putts. He took the putter back outside the line and cut across the ball, which is against all the principles of good putting. He always had the ball spinning a little from left to right. It just seemed to be natural for him to hit it that way. But he always hit it the same way, and he was a good putter for that reason alone." Bobby Locke, of course, did the reverse and hooked all his putts with almost legendary results.

Casper strongly advocates — and uses — an "orderly procedure" on the greens. He establishes and follows a set pattern for each putt, even to the extent of taking approximately the same amount of time to select his line. Then he steps briskly up to the ball, takes two practice swings (no more and no less) and then strokes the putt. Clearly, his orderly procedure is aimed at maintaining a repeating stroke.

Locke is another who has a set putting pattern, almost a ritual. He and Casper are much alike in this respect, the chief difference

Swaying is the cause of many a missed putt. If the body moves, the head moves with it, and vice versa. This changes the position of the arms, hands and putterface. Notice in the photos at left how the player's head has swayed to the right and left of the flagpole in the background, which has turned the face of his putter into an open position. Keeping the head and body still (check the head position against the flagpole in the photo sequence at right) makes it easier to keep the putterface square throughout the stroke.

between them being that Locke takes three practice swings to Casper's two.

A recurring feature of Casper's orderly procedure, and of Locke's near-ritual, is positioning the ball identically each time, and always getting that solid hit.

Achieving a solid hit is especially important when you putt from off the putting surface — from the fringe of the green, or from a short way out on the fairway, or even, occasionally, from a level lie in a shallow sand trap that has no overhanging bank. There are shots in which "touch" is a prime consideration. In these situations the first stage of your putt will be over terrain rougher than the putting surface. Since you can expect that the ball may be thrown uncontrollably a bit off line, your main concern will be to apply enough force to the ball to counteract the effects of the terrain. You should therefore be particularly careful to keep your attention on the back of the ball and your mind centered on hitting the ball solidly.

Jack Nicklaus explains how he plays this shot: "I'll nearly always putt rather than chip from just off the green if the ground is firm and free from wet or heavy grass. This 'Texas wedge' shot is

particularly useful when the lie is so thin as to make chipping risky. I use my normal putting stroke, hitting just a little more firmly than I would to cover the distance if it were entirely over the putting surface. One point I have to watch on these shots is head movement. It's a temptation any time you stroke a shot harder than normal to look where it's going too soon."

Most bad putts are caused by indecision. The player doesn't fully make up his mind how he wants to stroke the putt, so he changes his mind somewhere betweeen the start of the backswing and the end of the forward swing. He decides that he ought to play for more break, or for less break, so he changes his stroke pattern. Or maybe the thought hits him that he is about to hit the ball too hard or too soft, so he slows down or speeds up his stroke. The result is a wavering, indecisive stroke, and this kind of stroke makes very few putts. You must make up your mind in advance how you're going to stroke the ball, and stick to your plan. When the mind wavers, the stroke wavers, and a wavering stroke won't do the job.

Another danger to guard against during the stroke is becoming too anxious to see where the ball goes. Anxiety can, if you let it, make you raise your head before the ball is hit, which is fatal. The good putters don't raise their heads until the ball is partway along the line to the cup. They keep the head firmly in place and follow the first stages of the putt by just turning their eyes in the direction of the hole after the ball is hit.

"Some players don't watch the ball at all, but just hit it and listen to find out if the ball went into the cup. I think this is a good technique to use in practice, to form the habit of keeping your eyes on the ball and your head still, but in actual play it's very hard on the nerves," says Cary Middlecoff.

# part III
# special
# putting
# techniques

# 11
# lag
# putting

His Georgia neighbors glowed with territorial pride as Tommy Aaron negotiated the final holes at Augusta National trying to win the 1973 Masters. He had struck two shots at the par-four 17th, knowing that a bogey now could be suicide in a career that had known its share of self-destruction.

Aaron could sense the hot, competitive breath of J.C. Snead on his neck. He knew Jack Nicklaus had charged in with a 66 to keep his hopes flickering for a fifth Masters championship. Aaron realized, too, that any 11th-hour blunder could reopen the door for Jim Jamieson or Peter Oosterhuis.

All these things danced in Aaron's active mind as he gazed at the situation from the back of No. 17 green. He faced a scary, downhill 60-foot putt from the fringe. Too strong a tap would send the ball skidding well past the cup. Even worse, a lack of courage would leave him a treacherous par putt on the downslope.

"Tommy may not admit it, but he's probably the finest long putter in golf," says tour veteran Dan Sikes. "If I were facing a nasty 60-footer, Aaron is the guy I'd like to have striking the ball for me."

Aaron stroked the putt down the slick slope. It died 40 inches from the hole and Aaron, glancing back at the putt's trail, was delighted to be so close. He rapped the par putt into the cup and marched on to the greatest victory of his 12-year career on the tour.

"Very few pros enjoy being known for their putting," Aaron says. "It's not because putting isn't a great part of your game, it's

Tommy Aaron's amazing ability on those frightening cross-country putts — the 30 - 60 - footers that so often determine how well we score — has kept him in the thick of many a tournament.

just that you want to be known as a brilliant striker of the ball on all types of shots and not as a guy who continually saves his hide by knocking in long putts. But I'll admit I'm a good putter."

In this article, Aaron discloses his keys to those frightening cross-country putts, the 30-60-footers that so often determine how well all of us score.

# aaron on making long putts

☐ cut the putt in half
☐ visualize a wagon wheel
☐ finish with blade on grass

When facing a long putt, I am first a surveyor. To get the feel of the distance, I quickly walk from my ball to the cup area.

I check carefully for the slope and hidden breaks near the target. Many golfers concern themselves mainly with the overall terrain over which the ball will travel, but special attention should be paid to the ground around the cup. The ball will be rolling slower when it reaches that area and it will be more susceptible to contours.

Walking back to my ball, I will stop halfway from the hole and assess the putt. In a 40-footer, for instance, I will pause 20 feet from the hole. There I decide what the speed and break will be over the remaining 20 feet and I compute what I must do from 40 feet to have the longer putt on the correct course — at the desired speed — when it rolls past my 20-foot checkpoint. I'm simply facing a 20-footer with an extension. The ball will be going slower the second half of the putt and be more prone to break. It's easier to assess a 20-footer than a 40-footer, and my feel for the putt is better. I recommend lots of practice to develop a feel for distance in your putting strokes.

Once my surveying work is done, I stand behind my ball and try to mentally compute the intended course and speed. I visualize a circle the size of a wagon wheel with three-foot spokes that surrounds the cup. I just try to visualize the line the putt will follow and then roll the ball into that imaginary circle. Aiming at a large target, rather than a tiny cup, allows me to putt with greater confidence and with less tension.

If I do my job, the worst I'll end up with is a three-footer for my par. If things go better, it will be a two-footer or a six-incher. Of course, once the ball gets into the target area it just might plunk into the hole.

At rare moments of complete confidence, my mental picture of a long putt will include "seeing" it drop into the hole. It's a great psychological boost, and putting in great part is in the mind.

The preceding isn't as long and involved as it might sound once you make it habit. You can accomplish these preliminary chores within seconds, without becoming a candidate for a slow-player charge.

My advice after you get over the ball is: never change your mind. One of the average golfers worst errors is to erase all the spadework he's done and try to putt the ball on a new track at a different speed than he planned. That leads to disaster much more often than it leads to the cup.

A putt is visually different when you look at it from your stance. The break may change, optically at least. The putt seemingly may

Aaron does not try to hole long putts. Instead he aims for a circle around the hole about the size of a wagon wheel, figuring that if he stops within this circle the worst he will have is a three-footer to salvage par. To eliminate his tendency to get too wristy, he concentrates on finishing the putting stroke with his putterhead on the grass.

become slower or faster than before. Don't allow yourself such thoughts. Make up your mind before saddling up to putt — and follow through on your original decision.

As for the stroke itself, I don't advise copying anyone's putting method. It's an individual thing. I know I freelance a lot, changing my stance from open to closed, just searching for what is comfortable today. Putting is a "feel" thing. Do what suits you best as long as it produces results.

There are some basic steps in my method which I believe would be beneficial to almost all golfers.

I am not as mechanical as, say, George Archer or Bob Charles. I'm probably not as pretty to look at, either. All I'm thinking about is getting the ball into — or close to — the hole. There are no prizes for beauty that I know of.

I tend to get too wristy with my stroke, as do most golfers. Flipping your wrists on a putt doesn't really hurt if it happens after impact with the ball. But if I'm turning my wrists at impact, I tend to jerk the putt to the left.

There is a little training drill I employ to get away from overly wristy putting. I practice keeping the putterhead close to the grass until I'm four to six inches past impact. I want to try to finish with the putterhead on the grass. This gets me back to a firm, solid, repeating stroke.

There have been times when I've felt so confident with this practice stroke that I've used it through an entire tournament — I used it at Augusta. Most Oriental professionals use an even more drastic version, seeming to pop the ball with a short, crisp stroke.

Another characteristic of mine is a slight pause at the end of my backstroke. It's a split second when I get everything together for a good throughswing. It helps me slow down and smooth out the stroke.

Tempo and smoothness are a religion with me. Even the longest putt does not call for a robust, herky-jerky stroke. Feel and control are vital.

I won't guarantee that these guidelines will help you win the Masters, but they just might help you with a $2 Nassau.

# grip
# 'under'

Nothing is more frustrating to a golfer than an inconsistent putting stroke. Among most golfers, probably nothing is more common. A common cause of inconsistency is a wristy putting stroke, because to putt well consistently with a wristy stroke requires steady nerves and excellent touch, something few weekend golfers possess.

One cure for this malady is to grip the putter a little differently with the left hand, moving it farther "under" the shaft. This places the bones and muscles of the hands in such a position that it steadies the putting stroke. Arnold Palmer is one of many who have tried the relatively new technique.

In this chapter, Bob Toski analyzes how Palmer made the change and explains its effects. Toski, a former leading money winner and World Champion, is a member of the Golf Digest professional teaching panel.

## bob toski on arnold palmer's new grip for steady putting

□ turn left hand 'under' shaft
□ grip with all 10 fingers
□ feel 'one-piece' action

At the height of his career Arnold Palmer combined so much confidence with such a fantastic "touch" that he could almost have holed putts blindfolded with a baseball bat held behind his back.

In the new grip, Arnold Palmer's left hand is turned more "under" the shaft, to his left. This modification reduces wristiness and allows a smoother stroke.

That famous wristy stroke of his on the greens just went on working wonders year after golden year.

As a man gets older, however, both his muscular sensitivity and his nervous fortitude decline. That unfortunate process can play some nasty tricks on the pure "touch" putter when he gets under the kind of pressure Arnie exerts on himself.

I have always felt that Palmer would have been an even greater putter than he was if he could have developed a less wristy and thus a more consistent and smoother stroke.

In 1971, after 14 winless months, Palmer began experimenting with a new putting technique. The principal feature of this new putting style was gripping the putter with the left hand more "under" the shaft.

The great benefit of gripping "under," as this sequence shows, is that it keeps the face of the putter square despite Palmer's or anyone's tendency to wristiness. At impact the blade is looking squarely down the target line (see photo at far right).

The main objective of the change Arnold made was to diminish the quick wrist-break away from the ball that has always been a pronounced characteristic of his stroke, and also to keep the left wrist from breaking down during the putting stroke thus keeping the blade moving squarely along the target line longer.

Palmer received a big injection of confidence from the new technique, and began winning again. The "left hand under" technique has drawn increasing attention in recent years, particularly among golfers whose putting stroke, like Palmer's, tends to be wristy. Like Arnold, these golfers discovered a sense of stability in their putting strokes that had been missing since their younger days. With stability came confidence and a positive approach to putting.

Palmer has always had a very fast backswing on full shots, and that speed of movement began to creep into his putting backswing. The wrists would almost snatch the club away from the ball, causing jerkiness of movement and sometimes misalignment of the clubface as well.

118

To offset this tendency, Arnold first altered his grip. For almost all his career he has used the popular reverse-overlap, in which the forefinger of the left hand wraps around or lies across the fingers of the right hand. He dispensed with the overlap and began holding the club in all 10 fingers.

Keyed to this grip change, as a wrist-stabilizing and firming-up factor, was the location of his left hand farther "under" the putter-shaft — it was turned about an inch more to his left than previously. Take hold of a putter and try the effect of this yourself. First, hold the putter so that the back of your left hand is "square" with the clubface (as Arnold's used to be). See how easy it is to swing the putter straight back by breaking or hinging your left wrist. Now move your left hand "under" the shaft an inch or so and swing the putterhead back. You'll immediately feel less tendency to do so by hinging the wrist, and a stronger inclination to move the left hand and forearm back "in one piece."

By taking the putter back with his hands and forearms more in what I describe as a "one-piece rocking action," and less by hinging his wrists, Arnold undoubtedly felt that he could make a smoother stroke. Because the hand-forearm "rocking" backswing also is a slower and less snatchy movement than a wrist-break, a player feels able to swing the putterface square to the starting line of the putt more repetitively than by the old rolling or turning the hands or forearms during the stroke.

Arnie has always had a superbly stable head position on all his shots, and has kept his body very still when putting — absolute musts whatever type of stroke you favor. To give himself more freedom to swing with his hands and forearms, he set them a little farther away from his body than in the past. Combined with standing a little "taller" than he used to, this adjustment has moved his eyes more directly over the ball — another vital factor in "seeing" the line and stroking along it. In Palmer's case, the new posture also gave the impression that he was much more physically relaxed than in his old exaggeratedly knock-kneed, crouched, hunched-up stance. Less muscular strain and tension can only enhance rhythm.

My only criticism of Arnold's new stroke was that he didn't work his hands and arms as a unit as well going through the ball as he did going back from it. Most golfers should strive to swing the putter through the ball with hands and arms continuing forward in unison.

# 13
# the yips

## the curse and the cure

☐ don't second-guess yourself
☐ grip with hands apart
☐ change your stance

In the entire lexicon of putting, there is no more dreaded affliction than the "yips," an inability to execute a smooth putting stroke marked by quick little snatches that either scuff the ball a few inches or jerk it far past the hole.

The cause of "putting yips" is mysterious. Some believe it comes from a loss of nerves, others from a psychological block. Englishman Henry Longhurst, perhaps the world's best known golf journalist and commentator for television, believes that "once you've had 'em, you've got 'em," as he explains entertainingly below.

Despite Longhurst's fatalism, there may be hope for yippers.

John Jacobs, the well-known English professional, believes yips are caused by taking the putter blade back outside the intended line, in a mistaken attempt to take the blade straight back from the ball.

"When the putterhead returns to the ball, there is an involuntary effort to square the blade which usually causes a quick push to the right, jerking the hands into the ball," Jacobs observes.

"Once this is understood, the yips can be cured," he asserts. Jacobs advocates a "wall test" that those with this affliction can try at home or in the office. Place a ball on the carpet a few inches away from a wall and aim at a target parallel to the wall. In making a stroke, the putterhead should never be closer to the wall than at address. Most people, Jacobs says, find that they swing the putter

The classic photograph of the yips, according to Henry Longhurst, is this pathetic shot of Arthur Lacey, a one-time English golfing great. The left hand has flown off the club, the stance has become shaky and the short putt squirts wide of the hole.

back outside the line and hit the wall. Simply drill yourself until you are swinging back and forth without hitting the wall, Jacobs says, and your swing will follow the correct path and the chief cause of yipping will be eliminated.

If Jacobs' cure doesn't work, pathological yippers can try the cures offered by Julius Boros in the article following Longhurst's. Boros, whose languid, easy-going swing and putting stroke conceal a highly strung nature, has successfully avoided the yips through one of golf's longest and most successful careers.

## by henry longhurst

There can be no more ludicrous sight than that of a grown man, a captain of industry perhaps and a pillar of his local community, convulsively jerking a piece of ironmongery to and fro in his efforts to hole a three-foot putt. Sometimes it is even a great golfer in the twilight of his career, in which case the sight is worthy not of ridicule but of compassion. He will battle on for a year or two, but twilight it is, for "once you've had 'em, you've got 'em." I refer, of course, to what Tommy Armour was the first to christen the "Yips."

When he wrote a book called The A.B.C. of Golf, he had no

122

difficulty with the letter Y. The Yips drove Armour out of tournament golf. On a somewhat humbler level they drove me out of golf too, and a long and agonizing process it was, ending on D-Day, 1968, the anniversary of the invasion of Europe. On that occasion I put my 25-year-old clubs up into the loft with the water tanks, where they remain to this day because I am too mean to give them away.

Armour wrote graphically of "that ghastly time when, with the first movement of the putter, the golfer blacks out, loses sight of the ball and hasn't the remotest idea of what to do with the putter or, occasionally, that he is holding a putter at all." This confirms the description of that most distinguished of all sufferers, Bob Jones, who recorded that just before the moment of impact the ball "seemed to disappear from sight." Jones also recorded how he once was partnered with that sterling character of the late 1920s and early 1930s, Wild Bill Mehlhorn. Poor Mehlhorn. He was only three feet from the hole, said Jones, but gave such a convulsive twitch at the ball that it shot across the green into a bunker. He then had the humiliation of exchanging his putter for his niblick, and, we may assume without being unkind, that was the last seriously competitive round he ever played.

Contemporary with Jones and Mehlhorn was Leo Diegel, whose extraordinary spread-elbowed putting style put a new phrase into the golfing vocabulary — "to diegel." I watched him on the 18th green at St. Andrews in 1933 when, from some yards above the hole, he had two to tie for the British Open title. While his partner holed out, Diegel paced up and down, much as an animal in its cage, repeatedly taking off his felt hat and mopping his brow. When his turn came, he charged the ball down the slope, several feet too far, chased after it, and, almost before it had come to rest, yipped it a foot wide of the hole. Everyone knew, as I am sure he did too, that Diegel would never win an Open now.

Armour wrote, "Yips don't seize the victim during a practice round. It is a tournament disease." Here the great man was certainly wrong. My mind goes back to a conversation at Augusta with Craig Wood, who was robbed of the 1935 Masters by Gene Sarazen's historic double-eagle. Craig told me that he even got the Yips on the practice green, all by himself and with nothing at stake. Again, Armour says, "I have a hunch that the Yips is a result of years of competitive strain, a sort of punch-nuttiness with the putter."

Wrong again, surely, for you will see any number of compulsive yippers, though many may not admit it, in Sunday foursomes whose members never play serious competitive golf at all.

In winning the 1931 British Open Armour, having perpetrated a most frightful Yip to miss from two feet on the 71st hole, found himself faced with a three-footer to win. "I took a new grip, holding the club as tightly as I could and with stiff wrists, and took a different stance . . . . From the instant the club left the ball on the backswing I was blind and unconscious." Next day that greatest of golf writers, Bernard Darwin, recorded in the London Times that he had never before seen a man so nonchalantly hole a three-foot putt to gain a championship!

Who, would you guess, wrote the following, and in what book?

"As I stood addressing the ball I would watch for my right hand to jump. At the end of two seconds I would not be looking at the ball at all. My gaze would have become riveted on my right hand. I simply could not resist the desire to see what it was going to do. Directly, as I felt that it was about to jump, I would snatch at the ball in a desperate effort to play the shot before the involuntary movement could take effect. Up would go my head and body with a start and off would go the ball, anywhere but on the proper line."

That was written by Harry Vardon, winner of six British Opens and one U.S. Open, indisputably the greatest golfer that the world had yet seen. And the book was entitled How to Play Golf!

Americans sometimes refer to the Yips rather unkindly as "whisky fingers," and sometimes no doubt they are. Perhaps the last word on "whisky fingers" — and almost my favorite golfing quotation — was uttered by Vardon to a lady who was trying to persuade him to sign the pledge. "Moderation is essential in all things, madam," said Vardon gravely, "but never in my life have I been beaten by a teetotaler."

Sam Snead, whose fluent style has lasted longer than any other man's in the history of the game, was reduced to putting between his legs, croquet-fashion — and he was a total abstainer for years. The croquet putter gave many a golfer, myself included, an extended lease on life and the banning of it was an act of cruelty to many hundreds of miserable wretches for whom the very sight of a normal putter set their fingers twitching. The ease with which you could line up one of these croquet putters to the hole was quite remarkable. By holding the club at the top with the left hand, thumb on top of the shaft, and loosely lower down with the right arm stiffly extended, the most inveterate yipper could make some sort of stroke at a four-foot putt which would not expose him to public ridicule. We did not ask to hole it; all we wanted was to be able to make a stroke at it, and this we could do. The United States Golf Ass'n not only decided to ban a method which had brought peace to so many tortured souls but the group let its decision become public before the Royal and Ancient Golf Club of St. Andrews had time to consider it, thus putting the latter in the impossible position of either banning the club or falling out with the USGA. So they banned the club.

Further proof that the dread disease is not traceable to a dissolute way of life was furnished by the "Iron Man" of golf himself, Ben Hogan, who of all the men who have played golf since the game began would have seemed most likely to be immune. The rot set in, so eye-witnesses have assured me, on the 71st green at Rochester in 1956, when he was well placed to win a record fifth U.S. Open. Not only did he miss the three-footer, which anyone could do, but he yipped it, and that was the beginning of the end. At any rate, my last memory of Hogan in competitive golf is at the Masters some years ago. Every green, as usual, is surrounded with spectators and, as the familiar white-capped figure steps through the ropes, everyone spontaneously rises to give him a standing ovation. And a moment later he is stuck motionless over the ball, as though hypnotized, unable to move the ironmongery to and fro.

Is there any cure for this grotesque ailment? Few people can have made a more penetrating research than myself. The first led me to a psychiatrist-cum-hypnotist, who solemnly tried through my inner self to talk the ball into the hole. This, of course, was ridiculous since all I was seeking was that, on surveying a four-foot putt, a massive calm should automatically come over me instead of the impression that I was about to try to hit the ball with a live eel.

Better hope came from an Austrian doctor, who wrote to say that he knew the solution and would be willing to reveal it to me. Within a matter of hours I was visiting him in his rooms in London. "It all comms," he said, "from ze angle of ze right ell-bow." Something in that, I thought, recalling how, with the right arm stiffly extended, one could at least make some sort of stroke with the

125

croquet putter. The theory seemed to be supported by the fact that, if you have difficulty in raising a glass to the lips, it is when the arm bends to approximately the putting angle that your drink is most likely to make its bid for freedom.

What he said next, however, blissfully unaware of the full horror of his words, was "Violinists very often get it." We may imagine a silent audience of 6,000 people in, say, London's Albert Hall and the maestro in the spotlight, his right arm fully extended, drawing the bow delicately across, when suddenly, the elbow having arrived at the putting angle. . . . A-a-a-ah! He nearly saws the instrument in half and his career is ended. I once told this ghastly little story to Ben Hogan during a World Cup match and thought his eyes began to turn glassy. Only later did I suspect why.

Innumerable "cures" for the Yips have been tried and passed on from one sufferer to another. Looking at the hole instead of the ball; putting left-handed; putting cross-handed with the left hand below the right, and putting with the hands wide apart (probably the best bet of the lot). A friend of mine has his hands about a foot apart, with the left below the right, and then pulls down as hard as he can with the left and up as hard as he can with the right — and he a one-time runner-up in the British Amateur.

As an ancient and finally defeated warrior — three putts from a yard on the 18th at St. Andrews, and only as few as three because the third hit the back of the hole, jumped up, and fell in — I listen politely to all their tales. But the bitter, inescapable truth remains. Once you've had 'em, you've got 'em.

## by julius boros

I like to think that my best putts come at crucial times — that I'm some sort of super human that can withstand any amount of pressure. I'm not. Occasionally I have a terrible time talking myself into making even a 6-inch putt. I catch myself wondering if I can move the putterhead back and forth with any sort of consistency.

Rare indeed is the golfer who will readily admit that he or she is sometimes unsure of sinking a "gimme," but the truth is that there never has been a player who hasn't at some time or other lost confidence on short putts. It happens to the best professionals. So don't be ashamed when it happens to you.

To eliminate tension in putting, says Julius Boros, try changing your putting stance. If you normally putt with your feet wide apart, narrow your stance, and vice-versa. Once you decide on a line and how hard to hit the ball, don't second-guess yourself. Putt without delay, Boros admonishes, but don't hurry the stroke.

Through the years I've developed a few ways to shake myself out of these periods of insecurity on the greens. These methods usually work for me, and maybe they will help you.

There are three ways you can try to regain confidence in putting. They concern (1) your mental attitude, (2) your equipment and (3) your style. These all interweave, in a way, but for the sake of easy understanding let's keep them separate.

Putting jitters stem directly from lack of confidence — or fear of missing. This fear is most prevalent when a great deal is at stake. I think that is why most golfers get most nervous on putts that are very important.

To eliminate tension in putting you must eliminate fear of missing. You must fill your mind with positive thoughts, such as making solid contact with the ball or moving the putterhead along your line.

Above all, you must do away with any indecisions about the correct direction of the putt. I don't like to spend much time in lining up the putt, and I make it a point to always follow my first impression of the proper line. Those who second-guess themselves are really in trouble. Once you make up your mind about how you want to putt, set yourself over the ball and putt — without wondering whether or not you've made the right decision.

I do putt quickly. I'm not absolutely sure that's the best way; it's just my makeup. I like to get the putt over with before I can change my mind. There are occasions when I'm in such a hurry to putt that I don't give myself enough time to get a good feel for the putt. Nevertheless, I think it's better to putt in a hurry, rather than to stew over the shot.

Although I like to lag my approach putts, I'd just as soon hit the short ones firmly. When I try for a short putt I do like to imagine the ball riding right up to the hole and hitting the back of the cup. This is just another example of how I eliminate fear of missing by filling my mind with positive thoughts.

Sometimes a change of equipment can help you get back on the track. I'm not one of those who has stuck with the same putter throughout his golfing career. I'll change any time I think it will help.

Most of the time I will putt with my feet rather close together, almost touching. But if the short putts start going off-line, I might try a different stance. The change would be principally in the position of my feet.

Changing stances — like changing putters — is also a form of blaming the bad putts on something other than yourself. You blame your stance. That might not be the real reason for your bad putting, but the new stance gives you a fresh outlook.

There are many ways you can alter your stance. Pointing your toes in a little or widening your stance might give you extra steadiness. You might "see" the line better if you open your stance by pulling back your front foot from the line. One of these new stances might be just the thing to break that slump. If you start putting well, ride that new horse — that new stance — as far as it will go. Then change again. However, don't make major changes in your method. Just alter your stance enough to give yourself a different feel.

128

# 14

# side-saddle

Sam Snead, who has won more PGA tournaments (84) than any man in history, is playing as well as ever from tee to green at the age of 61. On the putting surface it's been a different story. But Snead, Golf Digest's Senior Playing Editor, has found a way to overcome the Yips and putt decently with his now-famous side-saddle style, which has proved more than a fad.

## sam snead's sidewinder style

- ☐ stand facing hole
- ☐ use left arm as fulcrum
- ☐ stroke with big muscles of right arm

The nerves are the first thing to go in putting, particularly among older golfers, but it happens to younger players, too. This happened to me about seven years ago. I'd always considered myself a pretty good putter, especially on the long putts. Then the Yips came, and that's an awful thing.

129

Sam Snead's side-saddle putting style is accomplished with the feet close together and turned slightly left, allowing the eyes to be centered directly on the target line behind the ball, which is played just outside the right foot.

The nerves that control the small muscles seem to be affected. I've seen people who can play fairly well but they shake so much on little chips and putts that they have no coordination at all. They might leave the ball 15 or 20 feet short, knock it way past or hit it way to one side or the other. I'm not quite that bad, but when I putt conventionally I'll push one, pull one, hit them everywhere but in the hole.

So I had to find a different way. At first I tried it croquet style, swinging the putter between my legs. Then the U.S. Golf Ass'n outlawed that, so I went to the side-saddle style I use now. I just use the big muscles of the right arm and shoulder, taking the little muscles of the hand and wrist completely out. If I didn't putt this way, I couldn't play anymore.

I recommend this style to golfers who have trouble with their nerves. You might not want to do it because it doesn't look like you're playing golf. But what's the difference how you roll the ball on the greens so long as you roll it?

The late Bob Jones once said to me, "That's a hell of a way to putt," I said, "Well, Bob, when you come in they don't ask you how you did it. They just ask you what you shot."

I used to feel self-conscious putting this way. People would snicker, but they don't snicker anymore. At the PGA Seniors tournament at the PGA National Golf Club in 1973 I shot 268, twenty under par and a 72-hole record for that course. I only three-putted one green during the tournament. When I got through, all those

130

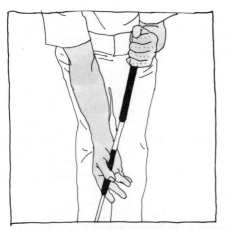

A close-up of the Snead grip shows the left thumb on top of the shaft and the fingers wrapped around it. The left arm is bent at a right angle and the left forearm points toward the target. The right hand is placed on the shaft about halfway down the putter, the shaft running between the thumb and the heel pads and across the base of the forefinger. The side-view of the grip and stance shows the left hand slightly ahead of the right. This allows Snead to hit down on the ball

older guys down there wanted to try my putting method.

It's awkward at first and it's difficult to get the putter going straight. But I'll say this — I could take a man who has a lot of trouble on the greens and teach him the side-saddle stroke and I'll bet he'll putt 50 per cent better after a half hour of practice.

If you'd care to try it, here's the way I think you should do it.

I use a couple of different putters, both of which have the shaft off-center from the top of the blade rather than at the end as it would be with a mallet-type or a pure blade putter. I'd suggest you pick one with a standard or a flat lie to better fit the stroke you'll be using. The only modification I make is placing a second grip (or merely extend the one you have) about midway on the shaft. This adds better feel and stability.

With the thumb of the left hand resting on top of the shaft, the fingers of that hand are wrapped around the club. The left arm should be pointing toward the target. If you make sure the arm is doing this, your left hand will automatically go on the club in the proper position.

The shaft of the putter simply lies across the right hand, running from between the thumb and heel pads to the base of the forefinger. The thumb should overlap the shaft softly. It should not close or grip tightly. All the thumb does is attach the club to your arm. The right hand should be very soft on the shaft.

The feet are together, turned slightly to the left of the target line. This helps you keep your body square and your eyes behind the ball. The left arm is bent at a right angle and, as I said earlier, the left forearm is pointing toward the target. If you get the forearm sideways and the left elbow moves out, then it's harder to stroke the ball on line. The elbow is close to the body but it definitely should not be resting against it. Your knees should be slightly flexed and you should be bent over comfortably.

The right arm hangs straight. Mine appears to be slightly bent but that's because I don't want it rigid. If it becomes rigid you lose feel.

The ball is played outside the right foot just far enough to allow you to pull the putter back without hitting yourself in the foot. (I've done that sometimes, too.) It is played three or four inches ahead of the right toe on putts 10 feet and under, about five inches on longer putts.

Both eyes are looking right down the line, an advantage over the conventional style of putting. You look at the line with both eyes — no closing one eye or other gimmicks.

You must putt with feeling and confidence. When you feel like you can make a putt, when you just know you can make it, you usually do. One warning. You have a tendency to come up short in this style of putting because you're getting power from only one hand. So make sure you strike the ball firmly enough. The stroke normally is made with the right arm and shoulder only, and only with the big muscles. I don't use the wrist at all. That's the whole point of this style of putting. However, the left hand actually controls the alignment of the blade. That's the hand that holds the club steady. On longer putts or when putting on slow greens I get added power by pulling the club back and down with the left hand. I've found this helps me get up to the hole.

Once you determine the distance you want to hit and get the proper line, don't look at the hole again. Don't try to keep the blade low on the backswing. Just swing it away, but be careful about getting it back too far. You can twist it off line if you do. Take it back as far as you would if putting normally. Remember that most good golfers don't take it back very far on the short ones.

Concentrate on striking the ball in the absolute back, trying to hit slightly down on it. I find the ball rolls better when I do these things. The sensation should be the same as if you were rolling the ball underhand. It's strictly a matter of feel, and you must practice enough to acquire this feel.

Once you do, I think you'll find the ball going in the hole more than you ever thought possible.

# 15
# plumb-bobbing

Dr. Richard H. Beers, the author of this article on the art and science of "plumb-lining," is a physicist working in nuclear research. He was co-captain of the Manhattan College golf team in 1962, and held a handicap between 1 and 5 during six post-graduate years at Yale, where he was twice runner-up in the Yale Golf Club championship. He golfs now at the University Village Golf Club in Goleta, Calif., and says: "As a putter, I'm a good physicist. My crowning achievement is having broken par while using 37 putts."

## how plumb-lining works

- ☐ find your master eye
- ☐ let putter dangle freely
- ☐ tilt body with slope

Although man has been around the moon and back, a distance of 500,000 miles, he has yet to learn to guide a golf ball more than two feet along the ground with consistent accuracy. This is not for lack of "scientific" effort. All kinds of devices and theories have been used in the unrelenting effort of golfers throughout time to master the apparently simple art of putting. Unfortunately, no technique has yet proven 100 per cent successful. It would seem that the problems inherent in rolling a 1.68-inch sphere into a 4-1/4-inch hole over a grass surface are greater than those of space travel.

Of the "scientific" techniques invoked by generations of golfers to improve their putting, one of the most common is plumb-lining, or "plumb-bobbing" as some like to call it. If you watch the professional tournaments on TV, you may have seen a player, as he prepares to putt, stand looking at the hole while dangling his putter in front of his face. He isn't invoking idolatrous spirits, or suffering from a paralytic form of the yips. Such a golfer is using his putter, as an engineer uses a weight attached to a piece of string, to assess the slope of the green and the amount of "borrow" or "roll" he must allow for on his putt.

Plumb-lining is based on sound scientific principles, and it can greatly help the golfer who has trouble "reading" greens by normal visual methods. To properly exploit the technique, however, it is essential that you fully understand its correct application, and also its limitations. A plumb-line by itself gives only one piece of information, which alone will not guarantee you 18 one-putt greens.

What a plumb-line does is define a vertical line, or, more simply, it answers the question: "Which way is straight up?" This awareness of true vertical is needed for golfers to consciously or subconsicously determine if the green is truly flat (horizontal). On many courses a golfer can determine true vertical from other sources, such as tall, straight trees or buildings. At the seaside a level horizon will indicate true horizontal. Given such backgrounds, plumbing is usually not necessary for most golfers.

Where plumb-lining becomes most valuable is on courses where, due to the configurations of background terrain, the true vertical — and thus the true horizontal — is difficult to establish. Many courses in mountainous areas fall into this category, as do layouts with greens cut into hillsides. Terrain that appears to be level in fact often slopes away from the mountains. In these circumstances — and others — a correctly-used plumbing technique can prove invaluable.

The first step in becoming an expert plumb-liner is to determine which is your dominant or "master" eye. You will find it easier to

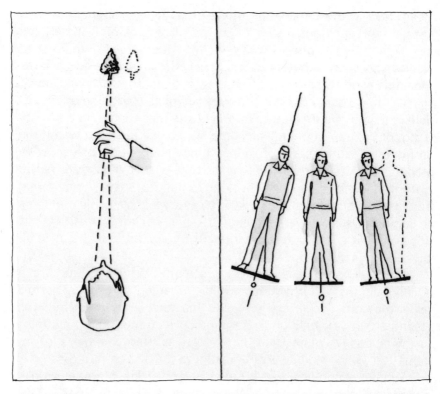

Plumb-bobbing must be done with only dominant eye open. To determine which of your eyes is dominant, first look at a distant object through your circled fingers with both eyes open. Then alternately look through the circle with first only your left and then only your right eye open. Whichever eye keeps the distant object in the circle is dominant. It should be kept open when you do your plumb-bobbing. When plumb-bobbing, you must make certain that your body is positioned at right angles to the slope of the green as is shown at right above in the more-detailed drawings. The ghosted outline figure demonstrates incorrect positioning of the body, which you should guard against.

make the necessarily precise alignments with this eye alone, rather than with both eyes.

To discover your dominant eye, simply form a circle with your thumb and forefinger, and, with your arms outstretched, look through it, with both eyes open, at some small, distant object. Next close or cover each eye alternately while still looking through the circle. With only your dominant eye open, the object you have focused upon will remain within the circle. With only your subordinate eye open, the object will appear to move outside the circle.

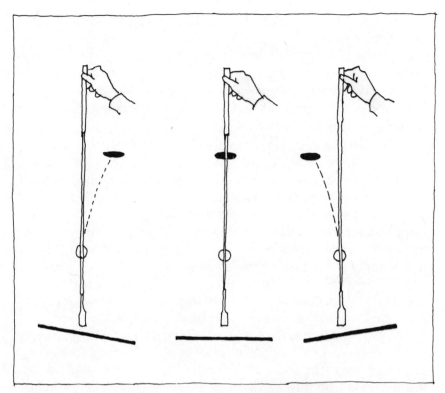

With putter dangling in front of dominant eye and covering ball, observe on which side of the puttershaft the hole appears. If it appears to the right of the club, you are standing on ground that slopes right. If puttershaft covers hole as well as ball, ground is level. If cup appears to left of club, ground on which you stand slopes left.

Remember which eye is dominant and keep only it open when plumb-lining.

The second fundamental of successful plumb-lining is to hold the club correctly, so as to establish a true vertical plane with it.

Take your putter and stand in the corner of a room. Hold the putter in front of you at arm's length, gripping it lightly between your thumb and forefinger at the base of the grip. Now, using only your "master" eye, compare the line of the shaft with the line of the opposite corner of the room. If you rotate the putter slowly, you will notice that only in two positions — when the putterhead points either directly toward or away from you — is its shaft in line with the corner of the room on which you are sighting. Note these positions so that you can duplicate them and thus "construct" a true vertical line on the course.

On the putting green itself you will always hold the putter — preferably by its grip end — so that it dangles freely from your thumb and forefinger. Gravity draws the putter into a vertical plane when you so suspend it. Be careful not to interfere with this force by gripping the club too tightly.

The next step in plumb-lining is crucial, but it can easily be mastered with a little practice and discipline. Place a golf ball on a sloping section of a green (or in your backyard if you are developing the technique at home). Now stand a few feet behind the ball, facing the hole or a selected target that could simulate a hole. Stand erect and assume a "square" stance (one in which your eyes and body are directly facing your target). Position your feet so that the ball is about 1-1/2 inch nearer to your left foot if your left eye is dominant, or to your right foot if your right eye is your "master" eye. This slight adjustment compensates for the fact that your dominant eye is not in the center of your face.

Now, here comes another crucial manuever. Imagine how the legs of a surveyor's theodolite support his telescope so that it is perpendicular to the angle of the surface on which it is standing. If this is difficult for you to visualize, try imagining how an ordinary kitchen stool would tilt if it were set on a slanted surface. You must allow your body to similarly tilt to follow the contour of the green (or backyard) on which you are standing. Your eye, the ball and the hole should all lie in a plane perpendicular to the surface on which you are standing.

Don't compensate for slope by simply relaxing your higher leg. Keep both legs fairly stiff and hold your head midway between your feet.

If you are standing close to the ball, the angle of your "tilt" from vertical should now be an excellent approximation of the slope of the green around the ball. The nearer you can stand to the ball and still perform the next set of movements, the more accurately you will be able to assume your stance, and the more sensitivity you will have to subtle breaks in the line of the putt.

Having taken the correct stance, lift your putter at arm's length, using whichever hand will hold it steadiest, and, gripping it lightly between thumb and forefinger, hold the club so that it hangs directly in front of your dominant eye. With the putter held steady, use your dominant eye to line up the lower part of its shaft with the center of the ball.

Now look up towards the hole. If the ground upon which you are standing is level, the edge of the putter shaft, the center of the ball and the center of the hole will be exactly in line. If the ground slopes to the right, the hole will lie off to the right of the top of the putter when its shaft is aligned with the ball. Conversely, if the ground on which you are standing slopes left, the hole will lie off to the left of the club shaft.

This follows because your eye, the shaft and the ball define a vertical plane which you are comparing to the plane perpendicular to the green at the point where you are standing. If the two planes do not coincide, it follows that the green where you are standing slopes one way or the other. You learn not only "which way," but "how much" because the greater the deviation of the hole from your putter's shaft, the greater the slope.

At this point I want you to learn how critical it is that you align yourself properly before attempting to "plumb" any putt. Having made a sighting correctly, shuffle your feet, shift your weight or move your head a little from side to side. You will notice that the position of the hole varies every time you make such a move. Next, step back a few feet and repeat first the correct sighting, then again change your viewing angle by moving your body or head. You will notice less movement of the hole relative to your line of sight than when you were close to the ball. Thus, the farther away you are from the ball in plumb-lining, the less sensitive you become to subtle breaks in the green. Both of these exercises serve to stress the critical importance of correct alignment if you are to get better information from plumb-lining than from the conventional system of assessing putts.

Once you have mastered the basics of alignment, plumb-lining can be applied accurately and reliably to better than 90 per cent of putts. However, it is the remaining 10 per cent that gives people who scoff at the technique their fuel for ridicule. These are putts having multiple or complex breaks.

You must always remember that plumb-lining will indicate only the character of terrain on which you are standing. If you plumb-line from a level part of the putting surface, but the green near the hole slopes, the plumb-line system will indeed tell you that you are standing on level ground. The hole will line up with the putter shaft. If you assume that putt is straight and play accordingly, do not blame plumb-lining when your ball finishes off line. This is a complex problem requiring a complex solution.

The first thing to do as you walk onto any green is to make a general survey and decide from that whether your putt is of the single- or multiple-break variety. This is easier to do than you may think; it is easy to sense visually whether a surface is warped. The more difficult problem arises in determining if an apparently flat surface is truly level.

If your general survey indicates that the green has a single, uniform slope, apply the simple plumb-lining procedure described above. If, however, the green has multiple slopes, then to properly establish the line of your putt, you will have to take multiple readings of the surface between your ball and the hole.

Assessing a complex putt by the plumb-line technique requires a combination of common sense and experience. For instance, a plumb-line sighting from behind the hole may give the best picture of how the putt will roll as it begins to "die." On a real helter-skelter green, it might be necessary to take two or more readings along the approximate line of the putt, using a fixed point like a spike scuff or a mark in the grass as a "sighter" in place of the ball.

You could, if you wished, measure the slope at any or all points along the approximate line of a complex putt, but, as a fellow-golfer, I implore you not to march around the green needlessly surveying every single blade of grass, further slowing up the game. In my view no more than two or three putts a round will need more than a single sighting. And, as I explained at the beginning, if the background to a course clearly indicates a true horizontal or vertical, plumb-lining may not be called for at all to determine the line of your putts.

To summarize, I believe that if you are an experienced golfer, or are familiar with the course you are playing, the conventional techniques of reading greens are scientifically adequate and practically reliable. If, however, you are a relative beginner, or if you consistently have difficulty in "reading" greens even at your home course, then it is worth giving plumb-lining a try — so long as you make it a fair try.

# 16

# reading greens

Few men in the history of golf have had the reputation for putting that Cary Middlecoff once had. When he sank an 80-foot putt en route to victory in the 1955 Masters, almost no one was surprised. Middlecoff certainly had phenomenal touch, but he was also a master of reading greens.

Middlecoff likes to tell the story of a man at his hometown course, the Memphis (Tenn.) Country Club, who had a problem reading the green in the finals of the club tournament. The gent in question, one Hunter Phillips, came to the last hole one down and had a three-foot putt to square the match and take it into extra holes. His three-footer was a tough little breaking putt, which Phillips surveyed at some length from all four sides. Twice he stepped up to hit it, then backed away to look again at the line. Finally, he reached down and picked up the ball, and shook hands with his opponent.

"You got the match," he said. "No way I could make that thing."

Maybe he choked, but a large part of his problem, Middlecoff suggests, was his inability to read the green and be confident of his putting line.

In this chapter, Middlecoff tells you how to read greens properly, what to look for and how to play the breaks.

# cary middlecoff's guide

- ☐ determine direction of grain
- ☐ speed, texture affect break
- ☐ wet greens break less

Knowing how to read greens is the mark of a superior putter.

The first consideration in reading a green is to judge the speed with which the ball is likely to roll. The length, thickness and texture of the grass, along with grain, are the primary considerations. Pay particular attention to the grass and the contour of the green within a three-foot radius of the hole. If the grass near the hole is comparatively heavy or if the putt must travel uphill the last few feet, go fairly strongly for the hole. You won't need to worry what the ball will do if it gets past the hole.

On the other hand, if the grass immediately surrounding the hole is thin or the last part of the putt is downhill, you should be extremely cautious.

Grain is similar to the grain in a piece of wood which indicates the direction of growth. Putting a ball against the grain of a green is analogous to planing a piece of wood against the grain. But while a wood grain is clearly visible, the grain of a green is often difficult to determine.

The best way to determine grain on a green is to look for shine. As you study line of your putt, if the green presents a sort of glazed or shiny surface, you know your putt is going with the grain and the ball will roll more freely and farther than you might suppose. Conversely, if the surface of the green presents a dull appearance, then you are looking against the grain and you must hit the ball much harder than you'd think at first glance.

Bent grass greens of the type generally found in the North and East are usually very grainy. This is especially true if there are mountains nearby, since grass tends to grow away from the mountains in the direction of water. Bermuda greens, such as are found throughout the South, usually have a more consistent grain. The grain found in Bermuda grass greens is frequently the result of cutting in one direction. It is also well to remember that Bermuda grass grows especially fast. Grain is even more a factor in the afternoon.

Grain affects the speed of a putt and the direction in which it rolls. Let's say that the green slants just slightly to the left but the grain runs in the opposite direction. In this case you should hit the putt directly at the hole because the grain offsets the slight slant of the green. The grain will affect the amount of break you should play — something you'll have to determine when you line up the putt and don your thinking cap.

Once they've seen the first putt overshoot the mark, many players become timid on return putts. A little nerve will go a long way in such a situation. You can usually find a good line on these return putts. When it rolls by, the ball naturally follows the line of least resistance in coming to a stop, and it will generally follow the same line on the return putt. So sight along the line the ball took when it rolled past the hole, make a very slight adjustment for your original error and stroke the putt with confidence. Where you are putting with the grain and the ball slides by a few feet, you'll be returning against the grain. If you don't consider this difference on the return putt, you'll probably fall short.

The contour and texture of the green, the grain of the grass, the force of your stroke and the distance of the shot determine the amount of break on your putt.

In most instances, you can see the slant of the green well enough to judge the break. When you're unable to determine the slant, the best solution is to examine the cup itself. If one side looks lower than the other, then the green slants toward that side. Sometimes you can decide on the break by getting well away from the ball and taking a long-range look at the whole green area.

Once you've made up your mind that a break exists, you should decide the amount of break and stick by your estimate.

Break depends a great deal on the force behind the putt. When the ball is travelling slowly, it will follow whatever break there is in the green. On the other hand, if the ball is moving briskly, its momentum will keep it more on line.

When the green is fast, play the full apparent break and try to let the ball reach the hole travelling quite slowly. But if the green is slow or you're in a match-play situation in which you'll lose the hole anyway unless you sink your first putt, you can risk a firmer stroke to make the ball hew to the line.

This problem of force vs. break arises when you're not certain

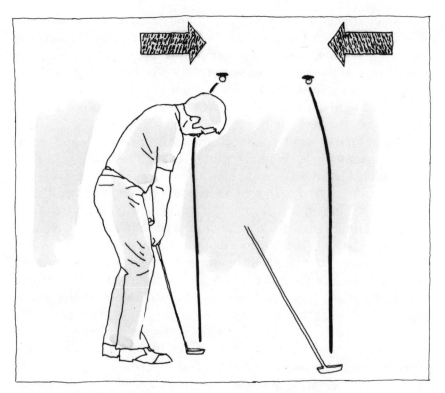

Putts will always break in the direction the grain is growing. If the grain is running to the right, the putt will break right. If the grain runs to the left, the putt will break left.

whether the ball will take a slight break or travel directly to the hole. If you decide to play the break, use only enough force to carry the ball over the front lip of the cup. Then if there's a slight break, the ball will take it. But if you decide to play the putt straight, you should hit it rather firmly.

That way it will hold its line against a slight break that's not obvious.

The greater the distance a ball rolls along a slanted green, the more it will veer in the direction of the slant. But we cannot assume that the ball will roll at the same speed all the way along the slant and that it will break twice as far on a 24-foot putt as it will on a 12-foot putt.

The reason is that the ball does not maintain the same speed on a putt, so the break isn't consistent. In the early stages of the putt, the ball will be travelling with greater force and hence will tend to

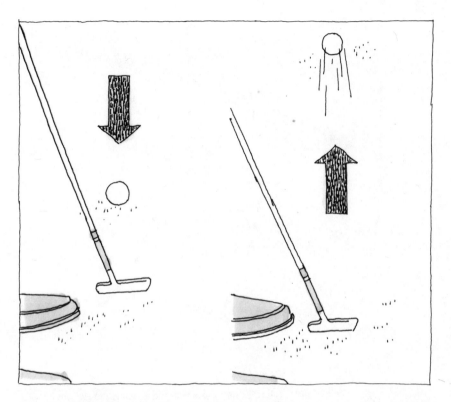

When the grain of the grass is running toward you, your putt will travel slower (left) than when the grain is running toward the hole (right).

stay on line. The sharper break begins when the ball nears the hole and begins to roll more slowly. This may be common sense, but you'd be surprised by the number of golfers who fail to take it into account when lining up a putt.

The green may show a sharp break for the first few feet and then level out as the ball nears the hole. Under such conditions, the tendency is to attach too much importance to the early break; the player allows for too much break and leaves the ball above the cup. The proper approach is to minimize the early break because the ball will have greater momentum in the early stages and will hold more closely to a straight line.

When the sharper break is near the hole, allow for the maximum break.   If the break is not consistent between the ball and the cup, always check to determine where it lies. And when it is

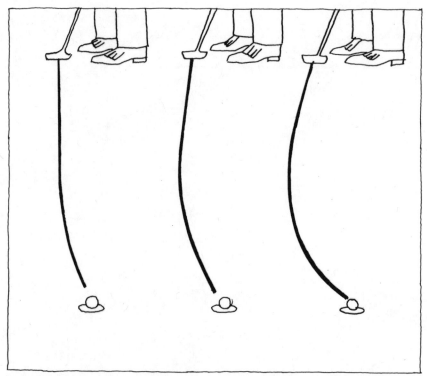

The rate of speed of any putt will determine how much the ball will break on its path to the hole. A putt moving fast (left) will break less than normal (center). A very slow putt (right) will break much more severely than normal.

consistent, remember that the ball will not take the break as sharply in the early stages of the putt.

You will notice that most good putters closely examine the final three or four feet because that's where the ball will be more affected by any contour in the green.

The final consideration in estimating the break on a given putt is the texture of the grass. If the green's texture is such that the ball will roll through the grass, the break will be less than it would be if the ball were to roll along the top of the grass. If the green is soft, and the grass pliable, the ball will run through the grass and there'll be less break. If the green is hard, the ball will skim along the top of the grass and take the full break as it appears.

You must play for much less break on wet greens because dampness slows the putt and reduces the effect of grain or slope. The ball rolls straighter in effect.

When the grass on the green has been freshly cropped and is slick, your putt will travel much faster (top) than it will on a shaggy green (below).

You must hit the ball with a firmer stroke than normal, which further holds it on line early in the putt. Watch for drainage lines and low pockets in the green where water accumulates. Bermuda grass tends to stay wet longer than bent grass.

The drier the grass, the more putts break because of grain and slope. This is especially true around the hole where the ball takes longer to stop than on slow "heavy" greens.

Once you have decided on the amount of break you can expect, stick by your decision. Never alter your plan in the act of putting.

On uphill putts it is well to remember that the back of the cup is higher than the front which gives you the advantage of a larger target. This also provides a little extra backstop, so you can stroke these uphill putts boldly.

On downhill putts, it pays to be cautious rather than bold. I

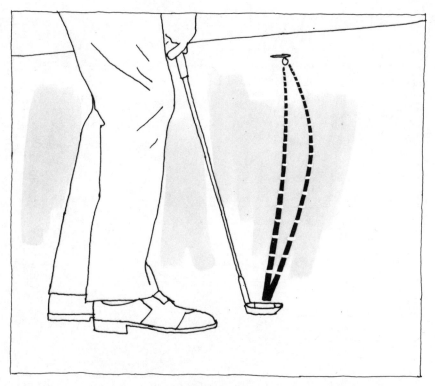

Play for much less break when the greens are wet. Dampness slows putts and reduces the effect of grain. On wet greens, the ball rolls straighter (dotted line on left) than it normally would (dotted line on right).

always found it best to play these putts to die at the hole. That way the putt would roll up to or just slightly past the hole. If I missed, the return putt would be uphill.

Sidehillers, I believe, should be played the same as downhillers — to die at the hole, or slightly below it. Putting boldly for the high side of the cup too often sends the putt far beyond, leaving a long, equally difficult second putt. Or it may stop above the cup, leaving a tricky downhill second putt.

A word of caution about "overreading" the greens is in order. Do only what is necessary to get a generally clear idea of the line of your putt. If it is a simple putt, deal with it simply and briskly. If it is a tricky putt, take a little extra time to study the situation. But deal only with the essentials. Don't go out of your way to add complications.

148

# 17
# common sense putting

Fred Taylor earned his nickname, "Stoney," early in life when he worked in New England stone quarries. However, his golfing companions, who give him any putts within four feet of the cup, swear that his sobriquet really refers to his fantastic accuracy on the greens. Taylor might have been a great player, but after he started manufacturing his "Marblehead" putters he neglected the rest of his game. He "researched" long hours on the practice green — he's stroked at least 1,000,000 putts over the years. In this chapter, he explains his technique.

## a fresh look at your stroke

☐ let left arm swing naturally
☐ don't lean on putter

Around every club there are always one or two guys who can putt . . and I mean really putt. He can't hit the ball for sour apples, but boy can he putt.

It usually happens that after you or somebody has played a round with this guy and he has got into your jeans for a buck or two, you get to talking about him (of course, he's already gone home —

you've noticed how those winners never stick around) and his putting. Maybe, you figure, you've found his secret. How he always points his left toe to the right of the line or something like that. Then another guy says that that isn't it, and then some guy always says, "hell, I figure this putting is about 95 per cent mental, anyhow."

You want to know something? He's right! But, before you can get right mentally, you have got to get right mechanically, even if it's cross-handed style. I've even seen some pretty good one-handed putters. Arnie does real good knock-kneed and Jack always pushes his cap bill up, but you can put your last bob on it that those two, as well as everybody else who can putt, have a mechanical reason which is sound for doing what they do with that stance or that grip or that cap bill.

Now listen to me a minute and see if this doesn't make sense. One of the biggest reasons for missing putts is fear, and fear is always present and will take over completely when there is something unkown. When you were little, you didn't want to go in a dark room because you didn't know what might be in there, and it was that unknown that scared you.

Therefore, if fear makes us miss putts and fear stems from the unknown, let's do away with that unknown by a thorough study of the mechanics of this putting business. Then we're going to find fear replaced with confidence because we'll know what we're about to do to that ball.

Okay, you say, you made your point Stonehead. Now quit grinding on us and make with that mechanical bit.

First off, we're going into a little bit of anatomy. I say a little bit because it wasn't on the curriculum at Reform School in my day.

If you will stick out your left hand with the thumb on top, you will find the hand will work only two ways from the wrist joint. It will bend from side to side and it will also work up and down, but it will not, repeat not, rotate. Any rotation must come from the elbow joint or shoulder joint. How about that!

Now then, get up from that big easy chair and take your putter in your left hand (right hand for you southpaws) and just swing it back and forth with your hand as if you were putting with only your left hand (right hand again, you s.p.'s). Notice that it swings back and forth easily, but if you want to twist it, or I believe I said rotate it, you have to do that from movement of your elbow or shoulder. No,

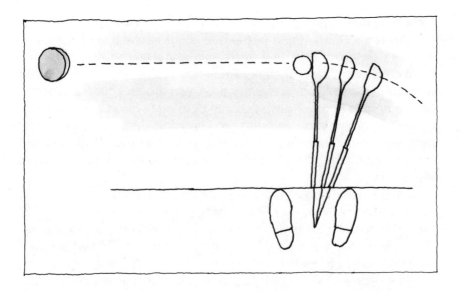

Stoney Taylor points out that if the controlling left hand does not twist or turn during the putting stroke, the clubface will swing back and forth in a natural arc which will hit the ball "a consistent lick" every time. He feels no effort should be made to bring the putter straight back from the ball.

it is not swinging in a straight line, nor do you want it to. Right here and now is where Ol' Stoney really starts to mess up your putting stroke.

Also right here and now, I am going to stop and draw a picture of you swinging that putter with your left hand (see drawing). This picture is going to be like my head is where yours is and we are both looking down at your putterhead swinging back and forth. And now we are going to imagine there is a ball there and the dotted line would be the line of a putt you are trying to make from, say, four feet on the last hole which will win all three ways for you.

Like I said earlier, the putter is not swinging in a straight line and it won't as long as you are not twisting your left arm and don't start trying to make it swing in a line straight through that dotted line to the hole. All that twisting and turning is why one day you can putt and the next day you can't hole it in Lake Erie.

In other words, the fewer false motions we have the more consistent we will become.

But Stoney, you say, that putterface is opening and closing and there is no way I can be consistent with that going on.

And I tell you that that putterface is not opening or closing, but is merely swinging back and forth in a natural arc which will hit the ball a consistent lick every time. And once you get to hitting that ball with the same solid contact every time, you are on your way toward becoming one of those guys that can putt, and I mean really putt!

But, you must be getting tired swinging that putter back and forth and you're looking pretty silly to your wife (husband) and she always figured this game would finally get you, so let's go over what we've been doing and saying.

First, I'm spending a lot of time here with you on that left hand bit and it's not just because I like to hear myself talk. The left hand is the controlling factor in successful putting. It will hit the ball a good solid lick and hit it toward the hole on the line, but it is awfully hard to tell how hard to hit the ball with it unless you're ambi something or other. I guess what I'm trying to say is that the left hand is the guiding hand and the right hand supplies the power and the "feel."

I haven't told you just how and where the putter should be held in your left hand and I'm not going to. You have got to figure that one out for yourself. All I'm going to say is to hold that putter so it will swing as we showed it in the little picture. I imagine you'll find that if your left hand is on the putter so that your thumb is a little to the left of center on the grip, then the putter will now swing like we want it to. Got it? I knew you could do it better than I could tell you.

Now, one other thing, you'll notice that if the putter is swinging freely you are actually holding it up a little bit off the carpet, or the grass if you are out in the back yard or the patio. Now put this fact down in your old brain box, so when you get on the course you will still be holding that putter so that it is just barely touching the grass behind the ball. I mean this is really important — hold that putter in your left hand so that there is hardly any weight resting on the grass. When the tension of the game comes on, and it will come on, don't forget this "lightly on the grass" bit, because if you get to leaning on your putter, you are going to ruin everything. Your balance will be disturbed and you will hit those putts real bad.

Speaking of tension — what we are trying to do is to make that tension work for us, and before we get off of this left hand kick (which it looks like we never will) I want to give you another clue which sure helps me.

Here we are with your trusty putter still in your left hand, swinging it back and forth and holding it up slightly off the carpet, grass or what have you, so now make your left elbow tight and still do the swinging. You know what that is going to do? It's going to put that tension where it belongs. Since it's going to make it work for you and eliminate any possible chance that your left arm is going to twist.

And now, by George, we are ready for the right hand, because we have built a machine with the left that will let that putter hang and swing no matter what that right hand does. It's just going to sit there and hold the line and let the right hand do all the hard work.

Since the right hand is the working hand, let's put all the fingers on the club by first holding the putter in the left (I know that's what you've been doing for the last hour) and lifting the index finger of the left hand so the right can get down as close to the left hand as possible.

When you want to feel something you use your fingers instead of your palm. Right? Well that's what we're trying to do with the right hand, so we grip the club with the fingers of the right hand. Now watch out for that right thumb, for it's the strongest finger of them all. I guess you call a thumb a finger, don't you? It must be. I've been doing my arithmetic most of my life with the five fingers on each hand.

Anyway, watch out for that strong right thumb. Since we've decided that the right hand is going to take the left hand for a ride and we have got the left hand set up to guide the putterhead pretty good, we don't want anything as strong as that right thumb in the act because it just might be too powerful and upset this smooth stroke we're building. So carry that right thumb real light on the putter handle, or better still, lay it over to the left of center and then just kind of pull the putter into the ball with the inside of the fingers of the right hand.

So let's sit back down and rest a minute and talk about getting that putter back from the ball.

The one thing I can't buy is trying to take the putter straight back, because you have got to make some kind of twist to do it and you might do it good on Wednesdays and lose it on Saturdays and this I don't want. A good putter is a guy who is consistent. You know, one of those guys who if he doesn't make the putt, he scares

153

you to death, because he's always got that ball in the hole or around it real close.

So, up on your feet and get the putter all set up behind the ball like we've been talking and let's put a glass — or one of those little putting cup gadgets — about four feet away and I'll just sit here and talk to you while you putt.

To get the stroke started you simply take it away from the ball with the right hand; arm, too, if you like. Now don't get it all complicated by trying to take it back low along the grass or on the outside or on a straight line or on the inside — just take it back — because that good old left hand with the club hanging in it is going to guide everything back in that same natural arc that we saw in the little picture. You have got to buy that stroke you just made, because it was easy and natural and it looked real good. All you did was to supply power and feel to that good old left hand hinge which has to work like a machine.

Do you realize what else happened? We haven't said a word about stance, but your stance was perfect. You just stood there motionless and nothing moved back and forth but the putter. All I can say is, you just can't beat what you just did. Just standing there relaxed with your toes on an imaginary line that was parallel to the line of the putt, without any weight on the putter to speak of (because you were holding it up off of the carpet just a smidgin). You just stood there natural like and made your stroke.

Well, that's just all there is to it from the mechanical side. There'll be a lot of things come up and some ideas and questions in your mind, but promise Ol' Stoney you will just brush them aside and go back and check on that left hand and see if it's hanging the putter good and not leaning on the grass. And make sure you're taking it back and through with your right hand and that the shaft is leaning toward the hole a little.

Well, there's only one other thing and that's what I call Ol' Stoney's prescription for better putting. I suggest you take a piece of paper and write a message to yourself on it. Be sure you read this message before and during every round of golf. Here are the magic words:

"I am the world's greatest putter."

# 18
# trevillion's method

A young British commercial artist named Paul Trevillion has been claiming for some time that he never misses a four-foot putt. Furthermore, he assures one and all that his unique method for holing those knee-knockers is THE way to putt.

"From four feet I could beat Bill Casper every day of the week," says the 32-year-old Londoner. "You see, Casper has a faulty method. He cannot guarantee every 4-foot putt. I am the only golfer in the world who can."

The British were typically reserved when Trevillion first began making his claims in the weekly Golf Illustrated, for which he illustrates instructional articles. But since then the vast army of England's club golfers, not to mention some tournament professionals, have become intrigued by the simplicity, and the successful application, of his unusual technique. Peter Willis, a British golf writer who covers the English golfing scene, has observed the Trevillion method closely and describes how it works.

## the man who never misses

- ☐ split hands on puttershaft
- ☐ crouch closer to the ball
- ☐ let master hand do the work

To try the Trevillion method, merely split your hands on the putter so that your left hand is at the top of the shaft, and your right hand — with the index finger pointing downward — is near the clubhead.

In Paul Trevillion's unusual putting technique, he places the right hand farther down the shaft on short putts than on long ones (see arrows), because longer putts require a longer stroke. Many of Britain's top players have experimented with Trevillion's method, but thus far popular use of the technique has been confined to club golfers. In the meantime, Trevillion has endorsed a special short putter, called "The Pencil," a move that cost him his amateur status.

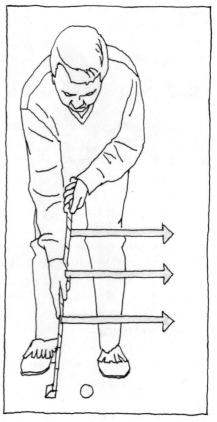

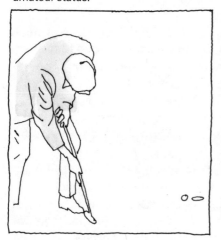

The distance of the right hand from the clubhead increases with the length of the putt.

The "stroke" is really just a push. Your right hand — your master hand — does all the work. Simply push your right palm forward, down the intended line of your putt. Your relatively untrained left hand merely acts as a hinged anchor and should be forgotten.

Trevillion says that some people who experiment with this putting style find that the pushing motion feels awkward at first.

This feeling passes after several minutes of practice, he claims.

Trevillion notes three advantages to be derived from his method: (1) It brings the player's eyes closer to the ball; (2) it forces the master hand to move the club; (3) it encourages a flat soling of the putterhead.

Trevillion evolved his putting style from watching top snooker players in action. He was impressed that they separated their hands on the cue and always had one hand (depending on whether they were right- or left-handed) as near to the ball as possible. "This is what gives them their precision control," he said.

"Also," he adds, "they get their heads right down behind the ball. This is why Sam Snead's side-saddle style of putting conquered his 'yips.' He has his master hand right down the shaft giving maximum control, and his eyes positioned as near to the ball as possible. He is right down there with the ball and this gives him confidence."

Trevillion elaborates on this increased confidence. "Stand on a table that's standard height — about 2'6" — and look down. A jump from that height looks fairly formidable. Now lie flat on the table and look down. It looks like you could easily roll off with confidence."

According to Trevillion, American professional Paul Runyan nearly stumbled onto the Briton's style over 30 years ago. Runyan was competing in the Belmont Open in Boston when heavy winds began to affect his putting. In seeking a method to stabilize himself, he anchored the butt end of the shaft against his waist, gripped tightly with the left hand at the top and extended his right hand down the right side of the shaft.

Encouraged by the results, he decided to test the new style thoroughly. From two feet either side of the hole he checked how many putts he could sink before missing. With his old method he made 143; with the new style, 400.

Trevillion takes up the story: "Unfortunately, Runyan discovered that the style proved a disadvantage on longer putts. His swing arc was limited by his anchored left hand. Instead of allowing his left hand to act as a hinge, he decided to use a longer putter and keep his right hand its normal distance from the ball.

"This, in my opinion, is where Runyan made his mistake. The reason he had sunk so many putts at first was because he dropped his right hand down the shaft near to the point of action — the putterblade. Furthermore, he got his eyes right down over the ball. By going to a longer shaft, Runyan pushed his eyes up too far from the ball and, in doing so, increased the mental pressure.

"Like Snead in his side-saddle style, I have reduced the amount of footage to be negotiated. That footage being eye-to-ball, ball-to-hole. I have barely half of the problem Runyan faced on a three-foot

157

putt. Like the person lying on top of the table, when I get my eyes right down there over the ball, a two-foot putt is unmissable."

In everyday life, Trevillion stresses, the left and right hands rarely work together. Usually the left hand steadies while the right hand does the work — knotting a tie; putting your coat on (it's usually your right arm you put in first), working with a garden spade, pressing a stubborn toothpaste tube and so on. When the left hand has to work with the right, people become "all fingers and thumbs." The left hand hinders, not helps.

"The same goes for putting," Trevillion feels. "On your weekend round you try to get the left and right hand to work as one unit. You're asking them to adopt an unfamiliar relationship, a relationship which has not been asked of them since the last weekend you played.

"What happens? The left hand becomes stubborn. It resists and you feel a tightening up as you attempt to knock in the pressure putt. With the left hand restricting the working of the right at impact, the putt is pulled or pushed to one side of the hole. I eliminate this problem of left-hand interference with my method of putting."

Another advantage of crouching down over a putt, according to Trevillion, is that it increases your chance of setting the clubhead flat on the ground at address. Explains Trevillion: "I believe that only one in 100 golfers sole their putters correctly at address, and I am not referring to weekenders alone.

"This fault is most common with golfers who wrongly insist that the correct way to putt is with a fairly upright stance. When a golfer stands too erect, he puts too much weight on the toe of his putter. The heel end rises above the level of the green. This destroys the balance of the putter. Even if the putt is stroked on line, it will seldom reach the hole.

"The correct soling of the club is one of the most neglected parts of putting. If you doubt me, take your normal putting stance in front of a mirror and check for yourself. I promise that many of you will be surprised by what you see."

# 19
# body putting

## exploring a novel concept

☐ slide hips and knees laterally
☐ keep arms, hands out of stroke
☐ aim correctly

One of golf's most sacred decrees seems threatened by the revelations of scientific study.

"Keep your body still when putting." That commandment has echoed across the greens of the world for centuries, with scarcely a whisper of dissent.

But now comes Vance Elkins, Jr., of Freehold, N.J., a seven-handicap golfer who invented the "potato masher" putter, then sought a putting method that would exploit its qualities.

The method is called "body putting." Forget wrist putting, says Elkins. Forget arm putting. Instead, merely hold onto the club tightly, with your arms against your sides, and move the putter by sliding your legs laterally, parallel to your intended line.

Several touring professionals, including Jim Colbert, adopted the Elkins method and began putting better.

Why risk the scorn of fellow-players by swishing your hips around the course? Elkins lists several advantages of body putting:

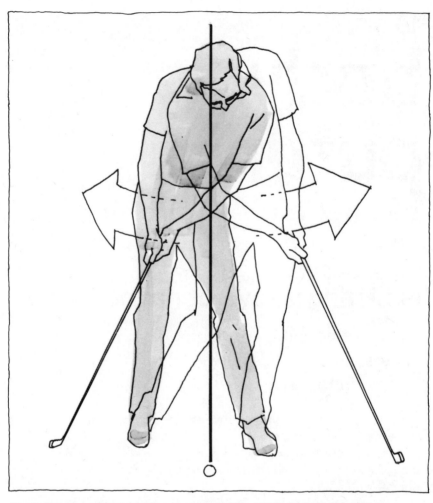

The basic move of body putting is a lateral sliding of the hips and knees in the direction the putterhead is moving. Ideally the hands and arms do not move independently of the body. Elkins advises that newcomers to the method anchor their elbows firmly to their sides to minimize any influence of the arms during the stroke.

1. It's the best way he's found to keep the putterface looking down the intended line throughout the stroke. He's tested various putting methods by affixing a piece of mirror to the bottom of his puttershaft, bouncing a concentrated light beam off it, and noting the movement of the reflected spot of light on a distant wall. When he opens and closes his putterface during his stroke, the spot of

light swings right to left. When he putts with the face square to the line, the spot moves up and down. He's found that various players he has tested invariably maintain a squarer putterface while arm putting than while wrist putting, but that neither technique begins to match the squareness achieved by sliding the hips and legs laterally, without independent movement of the hands and arms.

"The light machine proves that very small movements of the hands and wrists have a vast effect on the alignment of the putterface," says Elkins, "but gross movements of the body have very little effect."

2. Body putting is virtually tension-free. "I could be putting for the U.S. Open," says Elkins, "and I'm sure I'd experience tremendous tension in my hands and arms, but I know I could still move my body smoothly and make a good stroke. It's like a man running for a tennis ball; he can't be tense because he's moving his body."

A corollary to this advantage is that body putting involves a conscious squeezing of the club with the hands both before and during the stroke. With his hands already gripping tightly, the golfer finds it nearly impossible to clench or grab the club, and thus jerk his stroke.

3. Body putting gives the player great control over the power of his stroke. Elkins finds his body much more reliable as a distance-feel mechanism than are his hands and arms, which seem more susceptible to quick and jerky movements. He has tested this theory against several of the touring pros and, without fail, found himself better able than them to stroke the ball a given distance.

The technique of body putting is simple and straightforward. You move the club solely by sliding your hips and legs laterally. However, there are some pitfalls.

First, most golfers find it difficult initially to eliminate hand, wrist and arm action from the stroke. But this must be done. Combining hand and arm motion with body movement can send putts zooming past the hole.

Elkins suggests clenching the club very tightly at first, while forcing your upper arms against your side. In time you can reduce this extreme grip and arm pressure, yet both should remain relatively firm.

A second pitfall is the tendency to rotate, rather than to slide,

161

the hips. Any turning movement opens and closes the putterface, thus increasing the chances of striking the putt offline. Elkins feels that a slightly "closed" stance — the toe of the right foot aligned approximately with the ball of the left — encourages a lateral sliding, rather than a rotational turning.

A third pitfall, according to Elkins, is failure to concentrate solely on distance during the putting stroke.

He believes putting involves three distinct and separate steps. The first is reading the green, ideally from behind the ball. The second is setting up to the putt and aiming the putter down the chosen line (he feels you should never change your reading of the putt once you've moved from behind the ball). The third step is the stroke itself. During the stroke, says Elkins, the golfer should think only about hitting the ball the correct distance. He should never think about the techniques of the stroke itself.

"The path along which the clubhead moves has relatively little effect on the direction the ball rolls," he says. "What really matters is that you keep the putter facing in the right direction, and that you strike the ball with proper force. If you've aimed the putter correctly, body putting virtually assures proper clubface alignment. All that's left is the need to concentrate on distance."

Aiming the putterface along the intended line is a problem for most golfers. Elkins' tests of hundreds of players show that about 70 per cent align about two degrees to the right of their intended line — or about 8.4 inches on a 20-foot putt. Others align about one degree right of left. Only about 10 per cent aim the putter on line.

Most golfers, however, do not realize they mis-aim putts. Instead, they have learned subconsciously, to bring their putts back on line by manipulating the putter with their hands and arms while stroking.

Body putting, since it eliminates hand-arm action, deprives the player of this compensatory crutch. If he mis-aims the putter, then body putts, the ball will roll in the wrong direction. This will continue until he either forsakes the method and returns to his hand-arm compensations or, hopefully, corrects his aiming problem.

Elkins suggests that a golfer periodically ask friends to check his putterface alignment, both before and during the stroke. Once the player learns to aim correctly, body putting will help give him a repeating stroke he can count on.

# 20

# watch the hole

## putting with eyes on the hole

Keep your eye on the ball is another golfing truism that has been questioned from time to time. Recently, an Englishman named Hunter Diack conducted a practical test of this principle as it applies to putting. His son had made a small putting course on the lawn, using empty dog-food cans to make the holes. Since they were only 2-3/4 inches in diameter (a regulation hole is 4-1/4 inches), Diack found his putts had to be hit almost dead-center to drop.

It was in these circumstances that Diack began to question the keep-your-eye-on-the-ball axiom. Putting, he reasoned, is different from every other shot in golf chiefly because the distance the club travels is so short and the speed at which it travels is, comparatively, so slow. You should, therefore, be able to strike the ball accurately without looking at it.

"I wasn't really aware of all these things when I started my experiment, but it had occurred to me that in throwing a dart you do not look at the dart, but at the dartboard," Diack said. In baseball and tennis you must look at the ball, but in these games the ball is moving independently of you. You wouldn't, however, have much success in throwing a ball into a bucket at a fair if you looked at the ball instead of the bucket.

As a result of such thinking, Diack decided to compare two methods of putting — looking at the ball and looking at the hole.

"Even though there was nothing at all at stake, my feelings when I first putted looking at the hole instead of at the ball were of total insecurity. So before starting the actual experiment, I tried about a dozen putts in this new and strange way in an attempt to rid myself of this uncomfortable feeling," Diack reported.

Then the experiment began. He hit a thousand putts of between seven and eight feet with a 2-3/4-inch hole as target. The turf was not exactly what you'd find on the finest greens, and he believes that, if the hole had been of regualtion size, the successes — there were so many near-misses — would have been in the region of 90 per cent.

Altogether, he made 500 putts looking at the hole and 500 looking at the ball. He tried 10 putts of the one followed by 10 putts of the other. Then, when the thousand had been completed, he hit 100 putts straight off looking at the hole, followed by 100 looking at the ball. This was in case the constant switching from one to the other had had an unsettling effect.

"Let me assure you that I did my best, both ways," Diack said.

Here are the scores of the two sets of putts.

|  | Putts made looking at hole | Putts made looking at ball |
| --- | --- | --- |
| 1st Hundred | 28 | 24 |
| 2nd Hundred | 39 | 35 |
| 3rd Hundred | 43 | 44 |
| 4th Hundred | 42 | 41 |
| 5th Hundred | 48 | 31 |
| Totals | 200 | 175 |
| Percentage of putts holed | 40% | 35% |

These figures apply to the times when he switched from one method to the other after 10 putts of each. The following figures are for the 200 putts he took doing 100 in succession looking at the hole followed by 100 in succession looking at the ball.

| | Putts made looking at hole | Putts made looking at ball |
|---|---|---|
| Number of of putts holed | 54 | 39 |

Diack isn't certain that he has proved a theory, but he does believe putting with your eye on the hole is a good way to practice. Switching from one method to the other dispels monotony.

"What is more, I am no longer obsessed by the ball and that moving clubhead. Do I now putt looking at the hole when I am on the course? Sometimes, sometimes not — the habit of half a century is difficult to break — but I do putt with confidence both ways, and reckon that I gain four or five strokes on the round," Diack said.

One last word on Diack's method — if you try the looking-at-the-hole method, be sure to line up with as much care as you usually do. That will give you a fair chance of finding out whether it's better to keep your eye on the target at the moment of striking, or whether it suits you better to putt with the fleeting memory of where the hole actually is.

# 21
# emergency methods

## when everything else fails

Putting is an agonizing business, especially under competitive pressure. Most of the unorthodox styles shown here are efforts by touring pros and weekend players to prevent nerves from jumping into the stroke when the stakes are high. The styles look funny, but they may work for you, especially on those crucial two-footers.

CROSS-HAND     Orville Moody, pictured on the next page, is one of the more successful cross-handed putters on tour. He holds the club cross-handed for putts of all lengths — some pros use this style only on short putts. Moody feels that this method keeps his left wrist firm. He doesn't have to worry about his right hand "taking over" and mis-directing the putterface. Mary Mills (sequence) putts cross-handed on the ladies tour for the same reason. "I feel it's almost impossible to collapse my left wrist with this grip," she says.

166

She concentrates on moving the back of her left hand directly along the intended line "through the ball," a movement guaranteed to increase accuracy. The 1963 U.S. Women's Open and 1973 Ladies' PGA champion, like Moody, places all of her fingers on the club.

SPREAD-EAGLE There are wide putting stances on tour, but none so pronounced as Ruth Jessen's spread-eagle style. "I get good perspective on the line," she says, "keep my wrists stiff and putt with my shoulders. I know I won't move my body during the stroke and feel as if I can hit the back of the ball every time."

BODY LANGUAGE Once the ball is struck, you probably think you can't influence the putt. Wrong. Some great putters resort to body english, gracefully demonstrated above by Lee Trevino. Balance is everything here. Others, like Chi Chi Rodriguez, left, favor prayer. Often he traps the ball in the hole with a hat, in case an opponent's prayers also are answered.

168

BETWEEN-THE-KNEES    Kent Meyers of Portland, Ore., is shown putting during the Pacific Coast Amateur Championship at Olympic Club, San Francisco. Meyers and other practitioners find this style, which stiffens the legs and stabilizes the arms, more effective on short putts than on long ones.

AND IF ALL ELSE FAILS . . . if all else fails, you might want to punish your putter, as did Don Galka of Decatur, Ill. After missing a few short putts in the final round of an important local amateur tournament, Galka hitched the implement to his car and dragged it all the way home.

# part IV
# practice, rules and equipment

# 22
# practice putting

## how to build your stroke

☐ practice with a purpose
☐ develop touch on short putts
☐ practice concentration

Gary Player recalls that when he was a youngster in South Africa developing the golf game that was eventually to bring him all four of the world's major championships and a large number of lesser ones, he would practice putting for approximately two hours a day, about a third the over-all time he devoted to working on his golf.

If Player were starting over again, he would devote even more time to his putting practice. It is well known among the touring professionals that Player believes at least half of the aspiring golfer's practice time should be devoted to putting, basing his reasoning on the simple fact that a top player putts approximately as many times as he makes all other shots combined. Assurance of his putting proficiency also affords greater confidence and better morale to sustain other aspects of his game.

Player has doubtless noticed, too, that history's finest putters — players like Billy Casper, Bob Charles, Jerry Barber and Paul Runyan — have been those who practice putting the most.

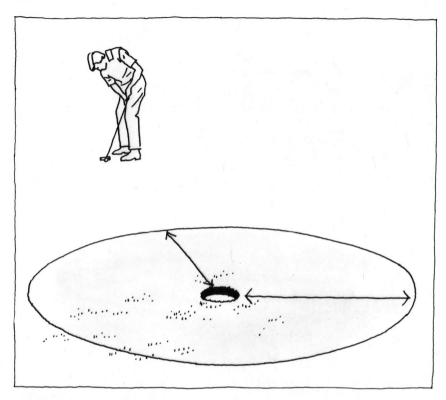

A good practice routine for long putts is to visualize a circle around the hole three feet in diameter. Practice rolling putts into this circle from 15 feet away until you can do so consistently. Then drop back to 20, 25 and 30 feet. If you can roll all your long putts into this circle, you won't three-putt very often.

No playing professional doubts the value of putting practice. In fact, it probably would be safe to say that no player could succeed on the tour if he didn't keep his putting touch sharp through practice.

Another point on which the pros are in virtually unanimous accord is that putting practice should be conducted along definite lines, with a precise goal in mind. They feel that it does little or no good to spend time on the practice green thoughtlessly banging the ball toward a hole. One who has developed an orderly procedure and who recommends its use to others is Billy Casper.

"Begin by practicing the short putts first," says Casper. "Drop several balls on the putting green about two feet from the holes. Tap them briskly into the hole, concentrating on the speed, not the line, since the line is easy to judge on short putts. After you have putted

Putting at a small target in practice is an excellent way to improve your putting. Horton Smith and Jack Nicklaus both have said they found it helpful to stick a wooden tee in the ground and putt at that, instead of the hole.

several minutes from the two-foot range, move back to the three-foot range. Then putt from four feet, five feet, and so on up to ten feet. You should select a flat putting surface for this exercise so that you can learn to judge distances properly. Putts that break should be practiced only after you hit straight putts of varying distances.

"Another common drill for putting the short ones is to first place a number of balls in a circle around the hole. Start at about three or four feet out and work around the clock, tapping each putt firmly toward the hole. After you have putted around the clock from this distance, extend the circle two or three feet farther out and go through the same procedure.

"One of the best methods of practicing long putts," Casper adds, "is to visualize an imaginary circle around the hole about three feet in diameter. Drop several balls about 15 feet away from the hole

175

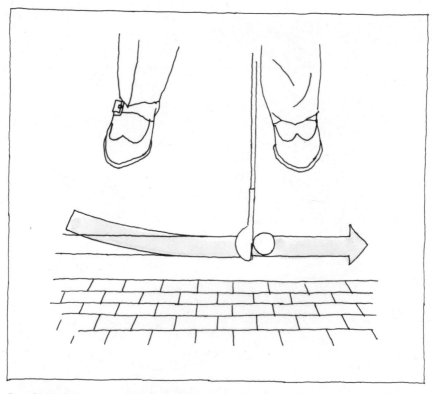

Practice building a consistent putting stroke with this wall drill. Address the ball about two inches from the wall and swing the putter back and forth so that it does not strike the wall. This will help you build an "on-line" swing path that delivers the putterblade squarely to the ball.

and try to roll the ball into the imaginary circle around the hole. Next, drop back to about 25 or 30 feet and go through the same routine.

"The important thing to remember here is to concentrate on stroking the ball the desired distance. Too many long putts are left short of the hole because the golfer has concentrated so much on the line that by the time he begins the stroke he has forgotten how hard to hit the ball."

Most experts agree with Casper that the best putting practice routine begins with short putts and works up to long ones. Jerry Barber, however, spends most of his practice time on long putts because, he claims, it better helps him to develop touch. There is virtually unanimous agreement that the main aim of putting practice is to develop a sense of feel for the power needed to hit the ball the correct distance. Cary Middlecoff, among others, advocates devoting a portion of your practice time merely to stroking a few putts along the green, rather than toward a cup. "This way you can perfect your touch and smooth out your stroke by concentrating on the cause rather than the result," says Middlecoff.

Horton Smith and Jack Nicklaus both said they found it helpful to stick a wooden tee in the ground and putt at that rather than toward a hole. The idea is that you can improve your putting by using a smaller target in practice than you would have in actual play.

Smith was also a firm advocate of home practice putting — carpet putting. "Practice during the off season will pay off a hundred times over in the achievement of better results in the spring," he insisted.

"Until the invention of ball-return mechanisms it was not much fun to practice putting on the carpet at home. But now the irritation of chasing the errant ball under the easy chair has been ended.

"There are also types of carpet that can be put down over your own floor that simulate very closely the usual surface of a golf green. Another important factor about carpet putting is that with very few outside distractions, you are able to forget about whether you are sinking your putts or whether you are up to or short of the cup, and can concentrate on the most important phase of your putting game — your stroke. That is to say, you can focus on your stroking technique to an extent completely impossible on the regular practice green.

"Work toward a 'discriminating' touch, one that can distinguish between a three-foot putt and a three-and-a-half-foot putt. I cannot overemphasize the importance of this, for it is here that you achieve the ability to make the ball 'die' at the hole. The practice method I have used for learning this has been to place two pieces of light string parallel to each other and six inches apart. Then I putt from about three or four feet away, first to one end, then the other, using about six to eight balls. You will be surprised at how inept you are when you first try this type of practice and how expert you become after you have worked on it for a few weeks.

The "wall drill" is a good way to build a consistent putting stroke, and can easily be done at home or office. Place a ball about two inches from a wall on carpet or another suitable surface. Address the ball so that the toe of the putter barely touches the wall. If your putter touches the wall at any point during your stroke, it is not following an "on-line" swing path. Learning to swing the putter back and through squarely will be relatively easy with the help of this wall drill.

Smith described another drill. "Blindfold yourself and putt to a glass tumbler from about three feet away. Put the blindfold up on your forehead while you 'square' yourself to the ball and your intended line. Then lower the blindfold and putt away. This is wonderful practice for helping you visualize a square-blade position in your backswing and also to help you rid yourself of any tendency to look up. With nothing to see, and merely the sound of the ball hitting the tumbler to guide you, there is no temptation to look up or to move your head as you hit the ball."

One point on which nearly all the experts agree is that putting practice sessions should last only for as long as the player can give his full attention to the matter at hand. They theorize that if you lose your concentration and start hitting practice putts carelessly, you will tend to do the same in actual play.

Jack Nicklaus is one who agrees with this.

"Over-practicing can make you a worse, instead of better, putter," says Nicklaus. "Your main concern on the course is 'feel'. That's what you want to develop on the practice green. When you've got a good feel going, quit practicing. Don't risk losing it by getting tired or losing your concentration.

"My objective when I practice putting is to achieve a fluid, rhythmic feeling between my hands and the ball in a well-timed stroke. When I get the desired sensation on six or seven putts in a row, I stop."

# 23
# art of greens- manship

## rules that can help you win

Golfers break more rules on the putting green than in any other sector of the game. That's partly because almost half the game takes place on what the United States Golf Ass'n defines as "all ground on the hole being played which is specially prepared for putting." It's also true because a great many golfers aren't clear about exactly what is allowed, and what is not, on the putting green.

Here is a presentation of the Rules of Golf regarding putting in simple "can" and "can't" form. As your weekend partners will most probably learn something from it, we suggest that you look it over carefully, too. There's nothing worse than being called on a technicality just when you were getting primed to accept congratulations.

For precise detail on any rule, you should refer to the complete "Rules of Golf," published by the United States Golf Ass'n and available from that organization, Golf House, Liberty Corner Rd., Far Hills, N.J. 07931, for 25 cents. The main rules governing putting are:

Rule 35, "The Putting Green"; Rule 34, "The Flagstick"; Rule 32-1, "Casual Water, Ground Under Repair, Hole Made by Burrowing Animal-Ball Lying in or Touching"; Rule 37-7, "The Player, Undue Delay"; Rule 40 and Rule 41, concerning Three-Ball, Best-Ball, Four-Ball Match Play and Four-Ball Stroke Play.

## LIFTING AND CLEANING BALL

You can lift and clean your ball, replacing it on the spot where it rested, at any time after it has reached the putting green.

You can't, in match play, refuse to replace your ball, after cleaning it, if your opponent so requests.

## TOUCHING LINE OF PUTT

You can remove any loose impediment on the putting green by picking it up or brushing it aside with your hand or club. If you accidentally move the ball while doing this, you must replace it (no penalty).

You can't touch the line of a putt — except to remove loose impediments, repair ball marks and lift the ball — other than to place the club in front of the ball in addressing it (so long as you do not press anything down). Nor can you "test the surface" of the green by rolling a ball over it or roughening or scraping its surface.

## REPAIRING DAMAGE

You can repair damage to the putting green caused by the impact of the ball, marking and lifting your ball if necessary to do so.

You can't repair damage to the putting green on your line of putt caused by shoe spikes, inclement weather or any other factor except the ball's impact. (This is one of golf's most commonly broken rules.) Deliberately tapping down on your line with your putterhead is classifiable as "repairing."

## HITTING FLAGSTICK

You can hit the unattended flagstick, without penalty, from anywhere off the putting green, including the apron or fringe.

You can't hit the flagstick, once you are playing from a spot on the putting green. Remember that if you choose to have your opponent or his caddie attend the flagstick, you become responsible for his action. You are penalized and not the opposing side if in this case your ball strikes the flagstick.

180

## DETERMINING THE LINE

You can have your putting line indicated by your caddie, your partner or your partner's caddie, but in doing so they must not actually touch the line "in front of, to the side of or behind the hole."

You can't place a mark anywhere on the green to indicate a line for putting, although you can use a mark already on the green as a lining-up aid.

## WHEN A BALL IS IN MOTION

You must replace your ball in its original position and replay your stroke (without penalty) if your putt is stopped or deflected, while in motion, by any "outside agency," such as a dog or a spectator.

You can't lift or play your ball while an opponent or fellow-competitor's ball is still in motion on the putting surface.

## WHEN A BALL HANGS ON THE "LIP"

You can, in match play, concede your opponent's next stroke if any part of his ball is overhanging the hole and you have allowed "a few seconds" to determine whether it is at rest. You may remove his ball in doing so.

You can't, in stroke play, wait more than "a few seconds" for your ball to fall if it is overhanging the hole, without risking being called by a fellow-competitor for an infraction of the rule against "undue delay."

## YOUR PUTTING STANCE

You can place yourself either side of the ball to putt and use whatever grip and stance you prefer.

You can't stroke from a stance astride the line of the putt or an extension of it behind the ball, nor with either foot touching that line.

## OPTIONS WITH OTHER BALLS

You can require an opponent in match play to either let his ball lie or mark and lift it, if it's on the green nearer the hole than your ball. In this situation in stroke play, you can require a fellow-competitor to lift or play his ball, as he chooses.

You can't refuse to lift your ball if, in match play, it's on the green nearer the hole than your opponent's (in three-ball, best-ball and four-ball matches, you have the option of lifting or playing it). Nor, in the same circumstances in stroke play, can you refuse to lift or play first.

## YOUR BALL MOVED, YOU MOVING IT

You can replace your ball without penalty on the putting green in match play if it is moved by your opponent's ball, or you can play it from where it came to rest. If an opponent knocks your ball into the hole in match play, you are deemed to have holed out with your last stroke. In stroke play, however, a fellow-competitor who hit your ball with his when playing from on the putting surface would incur a penalty (two strokes), and you would have to replace your ball even if he had knocked it closer to or actually into the hole.

You can't play your ball from a spot other than where it came to rest on the putting green, except when it lies in casual water, ground under repair, or "a hole, cast or runway made by a burrowing animal, a reptile or a bird," or one of these conditions intervenes between your ball and the hole. Then you can place it without penalty in the nearest position to where it lay that affords maximum relief, but not nearer the hole.

## PUTTING OUT OF TURN

You can require an opponent in match play who has putted out of turn to replay the stroke in the correct order, but he incurs no penalty.

You can't require a fellow-competitor in stroke play who has putted out of turn to replay the stroke — and he incurs no penalty, although his action, unless accidental, would be a breach of etiquette.

# 24

# equipment

## choosing the right putter

- ☐ it should feel good to you
- ☐ angle should fit your posture
- ☐ weight, balance should suit you

Many golfers believe that somewhere in the world there is one putter which, above all others, would be the best for them. They keep searching for it. They never pass a putter rack in a pro shop or a store without handling and critically examining everything in stock. They also take putters out of other people's bags and waggle them a few times before replacing them. If a putting green or a rug is handy, they conduct a brief test.

Some buy many different types of putters and keep them on hand for experimental purposes. Curtis Person, a Memphis amateur and frequent winner of senior tournaments, owns more than 150 putters, and during his career has borrowed several thousand of them. The trunk of almost any touring pro's car probably contains no fewer than half a dozen putters, and probably more.

Other golfers feel that the putter they have is generally suited to them. They plan to use it as long as it seems to work or until they just happen to find something they think would work better.

A few golfers swear that the putter they already have, and that they may have loved, owned and treasured for years, is the best one in the world. They couldn't conceive of parting with it.

Many golfers are convinced that a mallet-head-type putter is best. Others vouch for a regular blade-type putter. Still others prefer something center-shafted.

We might, for instance, on a given day in a major tournament find in the same threesome Billy Casper, Bob Charles and George Archer. Casper would probably be using a steel-shafted mallet-head which he had tested thoroughly and liked, but which he would exchange for something essentially similar if he saw any reason to do so. Charles would certainly be putting with a center-shafted blade that he has used for 10 years or more. Archer would be using a center-shafted, bronze-headed Ping putter. All of them would probably be putting somewhere between good and phenomenal.

There are a number of conclusions to be drawn. One is that the selection of a putter is a personal matter. Another is that it is not so much a matter of the particular putter, or even the type of putter, that counts, but rather of the player manipulating it. We should not, however, conclude that there are not sound principles upon which to base our choice of a putter, because all the experts agree that there are — including those mentioned above, as well as a host of others. As Bill Casper puts it:

"There are several important things to consider when selecting a putter. First of all, it should 'feel' good to you. Second, it should be balanced properly. You should be able to tell if the putter has good feel and balance merely by swinging it back and forth a few times, and hitting a few balls with it on the practice green. Careful attention also should be given to the weight and lie of the putter, as well as to shaft length.

"Select a putter that is easy to line up and easy to look at. Although putting styles have changed little over the years, many new putters have been added to the golf-equipment line. You shouldn't have too much trouble finding a putter to suit your particular needs and putting habits if you spend a little time looking over the various models."

Among the specifics Casper mentions are lie, weight and shaft length. So let's look first at these three considerations.

The lie is the angle of inclination between the head and the shaft, measured with the sole (bottom) of the putter lying flat on a level surface. The average angle of inclination is about 65 degrees. A putter with that approximate angle between head and shaft would be said to have a medium lie. An angle of, say, 72 degrees would put the putter into the upright classification, and an angle in the 55 degree range would give the putter a flat lie. Putters are available nowadays with any head-shaft angle you specify.

There is no real need, however, to know about specific angles, or even about the three general classifications of lies, because a set of simple tests will tell you what you want to know. Make the first test standing on a level surface. Take the putter and stand to the ball as you normally would to putt, comfortably situated, with your eyes directly over the ball and your hands as you would usually place them. If the sole of the putter is approximately flush with the surface on which you are standing, the lie is basically right for you.

But you need to make two other tests, because you will not always be putting on a level surface. Sometimes you will stand with your feet on a higher level than the ball (right-breaking putts), and sometimes with your feet on a lower level than the ball (left-breaking putts). For these putts you will have to adjust your stance position in order to reach the ball naturally and comfortably — feet closer to the ball for a right-breaking putt, feet a bit farther from the ball for a left-breaking putt. In making these stance adjustments, you will naturally decrease or increase the head-shaft angle.

You will notice that when you have to stand a bit closer to the ball, the toe of the putter will be flush with the ground but the heel will be slightly raised. Conversely, when you have to stand a bit father away, the heel of the putter will be flush with the ground and the toe raised slightly. You will observe that a putter with an upright lie would be better for right-breaking putts and a flat-lie putter would suit better for left-breakers.

To be somewhat technical about it, you change the center of gravity of your putter when you change its head-shaft angle. The so-called "sweetspot" (which is the spot on the face of the putter where the ball must be contacted to get an absolutely solid hit) will be moved slightly. When you move the putter more upright, you move the sweetspot nearer the toe. When you widen the head-shaft angle, you move the sweetspot nearer the heel.

To be practical you shouldn't carry three different putters

around with you and switch from one to another depending on the type of putt you have. What you need is an all-purpose putter, one that seems to set approximately right whether the putt is a level one or a right- or left-breaker.

One simple test might be termed the "coin-tapping" method. Holding up the putter with thumb and fore-finger, you tap with a coin along the face of the putter. When you reach the sweetspot, your thumb and forefinger holding up the club will no longer feel vibration from the tapping. Normally, the sweetspot area is located just behind the center of the club face.

To complete testing your putter's lie, hit a few breaking putts with it. On the right-breakers, contact the ball a little nearer the heel of the club than you have found the sweetspot to be. On the left-breakers, make the contact a little nearer the toe. If you keep getting solid hits, the lie is correct for you.

Most players like the sweetspot to be in the center of the face, or quite near it. But Jim Ferrier, a fine putter over the years, prefers to hit all his putts out nearer the toe of the club, so he has his putters specially weighted to locate the center of gravity in that area.

As to putter weight, the norm is from 15 to 18 ounces, with the head accounting for not quite two-thirds of the overall weight. Shaft lengths run from about 33 to 36 inches. Unless you are of highly

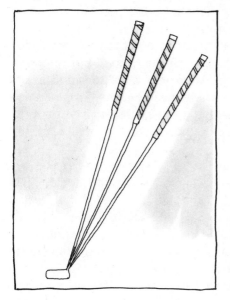

The shaft angle of a putter can vary to allow the golfer either an erect or more crouched posture. When selecting a putter, be sure that it suits your posture and putting style. You should not adjust your technique to suit a new putter.

exceptional build, the weight and length in the ranges specified above should be right for you. If you exceed these limits, you should understand that you are going against what years of experience have revealed to be essentially correct. Most pros use a 35-inch shaft length and an overall weight of 16 or 17 ounces.

Clubface loft is another important consideration. Casper has this to say on the subject:

"The question of loft has been a matter of controversy for years. About the only thing the experts are agreed on is this: there must be loft built into the putterface.

"Just how much loft is a matter of dispute, but I believe it largely depends on the types of greens upon which you are playing. If the greens in your section of the country are rough and slow, then you must definitely use a more lofted putter. This will enable the ball to 'move up' and ride high on the grass immediately upon leaving the putterhead. If you used a putter with little or no loft on greens that are out rather high, the ball would be driven into the blades of grass instead of on top of them, thus causing it to hop and jump on its way to the hole.

"If the greens in your area are smooth and fast, then you will need a putter with less loft. An experienced golfer, or your club professional, can tell you about how much loft there is on a putter.

"I would say that a putter with from three to four degrees of loft is suitable for all types of greens. If the greens are extremely fast, then find a putter with a little less loft to it. One of the major manufacturers of putters has determined that a putter with two-and-a-half to three degrees of loft will give the ball the best and most consistent spin off the face of the club."

In this connection, it should be noted that Bobby Jones' famed "Calamity Jane" putter had a face loft of 8 degrees, which is close to the average driver face loft of 10 to 11 degrees.

Another point to consider is that you should be able to see the face of your putter as you look down from the position of address, which you can do best with a fairly lofted putter, and which you could hardly do if the face did not slant back at all.

Bob Rosburg sums up his putter-selection theories as follows:

"What kind of putter is best? The one in the most confident hands. Professionals and top amateurs alike use a mixture of mallets and blade-type putters. No one type seems to be more successful

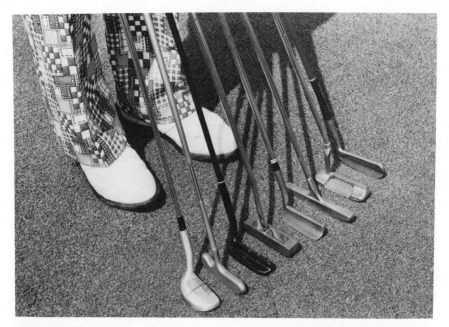

Putters come in a bewildering array of styles, colors and shapes. A few of them are (l-r): mallet, center-shafted Bulls-eye, modified Tommy Armour offset blade, center-mounted double blade, blade with thin flange, center-shafted long blade, Ping and the classic blade. If none of the above suit you there are several hundred others to choose from at nearest golf shop or sporting goods store.

than another. The main factor is the mental attitude of the player at the end of the stick.

"Over the years, there has been great progress in design of putters, just as with other clubs. However, I think the recent race to invent and market new kinds of putters has turned into a ridiculous competition of gimmicks.

"Odd putters usually have disadvantages that offset any advantages. Some unusual designs eliminate a great margin of error because the ball goes the same if hit anywhere on the face. But I find such putters, with their strange looks, different balance, and, often, odd noise at impact, cut down on my day-in, day-out effectiveness.

"I like a steel clubhead. Steel has a nice hard feel when you hit the ball. I have a lot of trouble hitting the ball hard enough, and steel seems to help me achieve a more solid impact.

"However, brass is a very popular material for putterheads,

particularly for small blades. It has a softer feel to it than steel. A lot of people like that 'live' feeling a 'soft-headed' putter provides. I don't.

"One thing some people find helpful is a line or a mark on top of the clubhead to help center the ball on the blade and help square up the face with the hole. I've never cared whether a putter had markings on top or not. I have enough trouble trying to hit the ball correctly without watching lines.

"Putters with colored heads seem to me to be more decorative than practical, but that's just another matter of preference.

"With a new putter made of shiny steel or brass it's a good idea to put a piece of black tape on top so it doesn't shine in your eyes or shoot off funny reflections. But older pieces of metal will be darker in color and won't give you that problem.

"Most pros use a much stiffer shaft than the normal one you would find in the stock of pro-shop putters. Again, the reason is to give the ball a much more solid hit without its springing off the clubhead. A limber shaft makes the ball come off much faster, a feeling that most good players don't like in a putter. Steel shafts are most prevalent. The old hickory or wooden shafts are not too popular any more, largely because they vary in changing climatic conditions.

"Shaft length is a matter of preference. Most pros use a thirty-five-incher. Just don't get a shaft so short that you bend too much over the ball. This is not natural and creates unnecessary tension.

"Most professionals use regular round leather grips on their putters. Some have gone in for form-fitted rubber or composition grips. There is also the so-called pistol grip which curves in slightly toward the player's body. This is mostly a personal preference in feel when placing the hands on the club.

"Personally, I prefer a rounded, soft-feeling leather grip. One problem with leather, as compared with a rubber-composition grip, is that you must keep it well conditioned to maintain its softness. I've tried flat-top grips but they just don't seem right for my hands. They are a help, though, for a player who wants to get his thumbs aligned on top of the grip.

"The diameter of the grip doesn't really make much difference. The size of the hands in relation to the grip is not much of a factor in putting.

Knowing where the "sweetspot" of your putter is located will help you develop a firmness in your putting stroke. The sweetspot is located near the center of most putters (center), although occasionally it is closer to the toe (left) or the heel (right) of the putterhead.

"If you are buying a putter for the first time, or have given up on your old one, start by carefully looking over the practically unlimited styles that are sure to be in your pro shop. First, pick one that looks good. Some golfers prefer the graceful blade, while others like the more forceful mallet.

"If you want to change putters, try using one styled completely differently from your present one. Once you decide on a specific style you can order one with the shaft length, flex, blade lie and grip best suited for you."

Billy Casper notes that most players who use the brisk tap stroke, like himself, prefer stiff-shafted putters. Cary Middlecoff, who takes rather a long putting backswing, likes a shaft that is stiff enough to have no play in it at all on short putts, but which flexes a little on long putts in order to help get the ball up to the hole.

Just as tastes differ widely in the selection of putters, so do theories on whether to change putters often, seldom, or almost never. The trend among the pros nowadays is toward fairly frequent changes. Many players feel that a change in putters will give them a fresh outlook on the whole putting problem. Some change after any single round during which they putt badly.

Dow Finsterwald notes that nearly all the tour pros keep more than one putter available for the different types of greens they encounter in various sections of the country. Following a similar theory, the player who customarily plays on his home course might like to have more than one so he can vary his selection depending on whether the greens are fast or slow on a given day. Once more, it is a matter of personal preference.

Against the fresh-outlook theory, you can set the perhaps more logical line of reasoning that the longer you keep a putter, and the more familiar you become with its feel and hitting characteristics, the better it will serve you.

Jack Nicklaus subscribes to this theory. "I don't switch putters very often," Nicklaus says. "I recommend that you find a putter that gives you the best feel, then stick with it. If you have trouble on the greens, the odds are 100-to-1 against the putter being at fault. More likely the problem rests with you. That's certainly true in my case."

The important thing is to select a putter that fits you, rather than altering your best technique to fit a putter. Dave Stockton offers sound advice on this point:

"Determine which positioning of your hands — high or low, forward or back, in close or out and away — gives you the best results. Then select a putter that "sets" your hands in that position. The best putter is the one that feels and looks right to you."

191